Natural Nutrition
for **Dogs** and **Cats**

Hay House Titles
of Related Interest

THE ANGEL BY MY SIDE,
by Mike Lingenfelter and David Frei

NATURAL HEALING FOR DOGS AND CATS A–Z,
by Cheryl Schwartz, D.V.M.

Natural Nutrition for Dogs and Cats

The Ultimate Diet

Kymythy R. Schultze, C.C.N., A.H.I.

HAY HOUSE, INC.
Carlsbad, California
London • Sydney • Johannesburg
Vancouver • Hong Kong

Published and distributed in the United States by: Hay House, Inc., P.O. Box 5100, Carlsbad, CA 92018-5100 • *Phone:* (760) 431-7695 or (800) 654-5126 • *Fax:* (760) 431-6948 or (800) 650-5115 • www.hayhouse.com • *Published and distributed in Australia by:* Hay House Australia, Pty. Ltd., 18/36 Ralph St., Alexandria NSW 2015 • *Phone:* 612-9669-4299 • *Fax:* 612-9669-4144 • www.hayhouse.com.au • *Published and Distributed in the United Kingdom by:* Hay House UK, Ltd. • Unit 62, Canalot Studios • 222 Kensal Rd., London W10 5BN • *Phone:* 44-20-8962-1230 • *Fax:* 44-20-8962-1239 • www.hayhouse.co.uk • *Distributed in Canada by:* Raincoast • 9050 Shaughnessy St., Vancouver, B.C. V6P 6E5 • *Phone:* (604) 323-7100 • *Fax:* (604) 323-2600

Editorial Supervision: Jill Kramer   •   *Design:* Renée G. Noël

This material has been written and published for educational purposes only. The reader understands that the author and publisher are not engaged in rendering veterinary medical advice or services. The author and publisher provide this information, and the reader accepts it, with the understanding that people act on it at their own risk and with full knowledge that they should consult with a medical professional for medical help.

The author and publisher shall have neither liability or responsibility to any person, pet, or entity with respect to any loss, damage, or injury caused, or alleged to be caused, directly or indirectly by the information contained in this book.

The first and second editions of this book were originally published in 1998 by Affenbar Ink, Kingston, WA.

Library of Congress Cataloging-in-Publication Data

Schultze, Kymythy R.
     Natural nutrition for dogs and cats : the ultimate diet / Kymythy R. Schultze.
         p.   cm.
     ISBN 1-56170-636-1 (tradepaper)
     1. Dogs—Nutrition.   2. Cats—Nutrition.   3. Dogs—Food.   4. Cats—Food.   5. Dogs—Diseases—Diet therapy.   6. Cats—Diseases—Diet therapy.   I. Title.
SF427.4.S3   1999
636.7'084—dc21

                                                99–23629
                                                CIP

ISBN 13: 978-1-56170-636-5
ISBN 10: 1-56170-636-1

07 06 05 04   13 12 11 10
First printing, Hay House edition, October 1999
10th printing, November 2004

Printed in Canada

For my beloved Liesel

❧ ❧ ❧

Thank you . . .

*To Mom: for nurturing my love of animals
(even the slimy ones)
To Blair: for your unconditional love
To Claire: for your friendship and guidance
To Richard: for saving my life*

and

*To my furry friends:
for your patience and skill in teaching me
how to care for you*

✒ Contents ✒

✍ *Foreword* ✍

by Louise L. Hay

"This is vital information that needs to reach every pet-lover as soon as possible."

The well-being of our furry friends has always been very important to me.

I don't buy animals; I rescue them from shelters. My only criteria for dogs is that they are female and under 20 pounds. In the past several years, I have wound up with four pedigreed dogs: Winkie, a mini-dachshund; Hyland, a West Highland terrier; Frances, a Scottish terrier; and Billy Boy, a Lhasa Apso. The main reason I like small dogs is that if they misbehave or create a problem, I just pick them up and the situation is ended. I can't do that with a large dog.

Knowing for years that commercial pet food is some of the worst of junk foods, I had always cooked what I believed was healthy food for my animals: brown rice with vegetables and meat. I cooked large batches every few weeks and froze them in portion-sized containers. Current commercial pet food keeps veterinarians busy as they struggle to heal diseases they don't know how to treat. The pharmaceutical industry is killing our pets with medications—yet all they need is healthy food.

One day I saw an ad for a workshop called "Natural Nutrition for Dogs and Cats." This intrigued me, and my inner self said, *Go check this out.* So I did. The first thing I saw when I entered the room was a magnificent Newfoundland who turned out be the canine companion of Kymythy Schultze, the leader of the workshop. Panda was loving and friendly, with a shining coat and clean teeth, and she smelled delicious. I fell in love with this dog immediately. Whatever she was eating had to be good for her.

Kymythy told us, "Remember, dogs and cats are carnivores, and in the wild, no animal cooks its food. Your domesticated animal needs species-appropriate nutrition to achieve optimum health." I thought, *Of course, it's so simple. Why didn't I think of it before?*

I continued to nod my head for the next two hours as she continued to explain the simplicity and ease of bringing our animals back to perfect health. I bought her self-published book, took it home, and read it two or three times.

Even though I had taken the best care of my dogs that I knew how to, three of them had succumbed to a variety of diseases. They were then buried in a small pet cemetery I had in my garden. I planted a beautiful flowering shrub over each grave as a reminder of how wonderful they were. Frances had heather; Billy Boy, lavender; Winkie, lion's ears; and Sabrina the cat, Mexican marigold. So at this point, the only dog I have left is Hyland.

The first day I began feeding Hyland the new diet, I gave her two-thirds of her regular food mixed with one-third raw meat. The second day I added more raw meat, and by the third day Hyland was joyfully eating this new diet. This was a dog who used to have such severe skin problems that she would dig a hole in her back trying to escape the intense itching. Within three days, she stopped itching. The wound in her back healed, and her coat began to grow.

Within two weeks, her coat was starting to shine, and she had much more energy than she'd had in years. This was a younger, healthy dog. I was convinced. I was also sorry I hadn't known about it for my other animals while they were still alive.

Hyland's diet evolved. She began to enjoy a chicken wing or neck for breakfast, chopped into chunks rather than whole. For dinner she enjoyed ground beef, chicken, or turkey, occasionally with raw beef stew, all mixed with finely chopped raw vegetables. A little flaxseed oil and some mixed alfalfa powder, vitamin C, and kelp made the meal complete.

To make preparation simple, I would order eight-pound bags of chicken wings or necks from the butcher, and buy several pounds of ground meat at a time. I would then separate the wings and meat into portions and freeze them in small plastic bags. Each night I take out one chicken neck and one bag of meat. By morning they are thawed in the fridge. Couldn't be simpler.

I began to share this diet with some friends. Those who were willing to try were amazed at the positive results. Some of the dogs reacted as though they had been waiting for a decent meal all their lives. One friend told me that her dog took one look at the chicken wing offered for breakfast, grabbed it, took it into the living room, threw it up in the air, caught it, and gobbled it down. Over and over I heard friends say, "Thank you for giving me back my dogs. They have so much energy now."

Kymythy Schultze is a wonderful, dedicated woman who truly cares about our furry friends. Her book is invaluable; her workshops, enlightening. However, she can only reach so many people at a time, and this is vital information that needs to reach every pet lover as soon as possible. I approached Kymythy with the idea that she allow Hay House to publish her book so that she could have widespread distribution. When Kymythy agreed, I almost wept with joy. Now we can bring natural healing for animals to everyone who is open to serving the healthiest food to their pets.

A few months ago, I mentioned this diet in one of my *Dear Louise* advice columns. The response has been overwhelming.

As a publisher, I am proud to present this book!

✥ *Foreword* ✥

by Bruce W. Cauble, D.V.M.

"Natural Nutrition for Dogs and Cats is an excellent
starting point for us all."

After graduating from the University of California at Davis School of Veterinary Medicine in 1970, I became concerned about the lack of research on nutrition for dogs and cats. Veterinary research at that time was focused on the diagnosis and pharmaceutical treatment of diseases, with little attention to exploring diet as a potential cause of disease or as a component of treatment protocols. We simply assumed that the pet food industry had done the necessary research and were thus providing us with "optimum" diets for our patients.

As an undergraduate, I had developed an interest in human and animal nutrition and received a degree in animal nutrition and physiology. This interest led me to a seminar by Jeffrey Bland, Ph.D., a researcher whose work emphasized the bioavailability [AUTHOR'S NOTE: *bioavailability* means "the ability to be of use to a living organism"] of nutrients and antioxidants, and their use in the treatment of degenerative diseases. Soon after, I began recommending vitamin and mineral supplements for dogs with arthritis. Within a month, I observed a considerable improvement in at least 75 percent of the animals supplemented. I theorized that either something had previously been missing in the dogs' diets or that vital nutrients were somehow being changed through processing, and thus made unavailable to the body during digestion.

This experience inspired me to conduct a bit of personal research into the pet food industry. I learned that a large number of commercial diets were formulated and prepared from a list of nutrients considered necessary for the health of dogs and cats, but no feeding trials were conducted to test these products, and more important, no assays had been done to check the bioavailability of critical nutrients after cooking, processing, and packaging. The ingredient list on the side of the package might look impressive, but if your pet cannot digest and absorb the nutrients inside, they are of no value.

Before commercially prepared diets became available, our pets fed on leftovers and whatever else they could find. They often ate fresh whole food off the ground, which added small amounts of trace nutrients to their diet. Today, however, we feed them highly processed diets out of dishes, thus eliminating any opportunity for them to supplement their diet with missing nutrients.

In the early 1980s, alternative health care for pets began to flourish, and I became involved in a number of "holistic" veterinary organizations. Unfortunately, however, most of the other individuals participating in these groups were vegetarians who thought it appropriate to develop vegetarian diets for their fanged, carnivorous friends. Logic and common sense are critical to good science. Animals, just like people, are still using digestive systems that evolved thousands of years ago, systems designed to provide us with nutrients derived from whole foods. You need only look at the digestive system of an organism to determine its appropriate diet. Our "captive" companion friends, designed as meat eaters, rely on us to use some logic and common sense in caring for them.

Kymythy Schultze understands this important concept. I first met her about ten years ago as a client coming to my practice for a "dietary consult." At the time, the majority of my clients were holistic-minded; they expected me, as a holistic veterinarian, to recommend a non-meat diet to cure their pets' problems. I often spent hours trying to convince these individuals that dogs and cats are by nature carnivores, not vegetarians. I showed them photographs and lab reports documenting how poorly dogs and cats did on non-meat diets. And I routinely observed anemia, poor hair coats, poor bone development, enlarged hearts, low serum protein levels, lethargy, poor immune response, and even seizures in these animals. Kymythy was an exception to that trend. While most of my clients brought me animals in various stages of disrepair, Kymythy presented me with beautiful, healthy dogs and wanted to know how I felt about the diet she fed them, which was based on raw meat. Real carnivore food. Logic and common sense had prevailed.

As we see in the human health arena, nutrition is finally coming of age. The links between improper diet and numerous diseases such as cancer, arthritis, diabetes, and heart disease are now well documented. Experts are urging us to eat more fresh, whole foods and fewer processed products. It's time we began to respect the dietary needs of our pets as well as ourselves.

Over the past 20 years, Kymythy has made it her mission to learn all that she can about nutrition and health care. She has now assembled this information in this easy-to-read, easy-to-do book designed to help us meet our animals' optimal nutritional needs.

Natural Nutrition for Dogs and Cats is an excellent starting point for us all. Its pages are filled with helpful hints, good advice and, most important, logic and common sense.

ᲔᲠ *Foreword* ᲔᲠ

by Stephen R. Blake, Jr., D.V.M.

"The purpose of this book is simply to introduce you to a healthier lifestyle for your pets."

In my 24 years as a holistic veterinary practitioner, I've found that optimum nutrition is the foundation for all methods of healing, whether alternative or conventional. In these pages, Kymythy Schultze has provided an excellent nutritional text to help us build a healthier life for our animal friends.

"Who is Kymythy Schultze?" you may be asking. My answer to that begins 20 years ago when I saw a skeptical pet lover introduced to alternative veterinary medicine. Over the past 20 years, she has become a student and teacher of that which she once questioned, studying animal training, nutrition, and health care. Kymythy is now a qualified animal nutritionist and is certified by the state of California as an Animal Health Instructor. In addition, she is energetic and dedicated to her beliefs, and she practices what she preaches. I have worked with her pets over these many years and seen the benefits of her natural feeding in conjunction with holistic veterinary care.

The concept of raw food diets is not a new topic. But in this book, Kymythy offers a simple explanation of the importance of raw food and addresses many of the concerns pet owners have about making their own pet food. You will find here both humor and solid information about the potential benefits of the raw-food approach for your animals' optimum health. This text is by no means the answer to all of your pets' health needs, but it provides an excellent foundation for building a healthier immune system to help your animals deal with the stresses of a polluted world.

The purpose of this book is simply to introduce you to a healthier lifestyle for your pets. Use it as a stepping stone to learn more about what you can do to help prevent health problems in your animals before they begin.

❧ *Introduction* ❧

The information contained herein may not appeal to every animal lover because there are as many different ways to feed cats and dogs as there are people doing it. This book was not written to force anyone into doing something that they are not comfortable with. It was written for people who are interested in feeding a healthy, homemade diet to their animal companions. After much research and experimentation, I first made this information available to my puppies' families in 1991. This edition has been expanded to include cats and all breeds of dogs. It is the sort of book that I wished was available when I first started my journey into animal nutrition.

Natural Nutrition for Dogs and Cats: The Ultimate Diet was written by popular request. The students in my "Natural Nutrition for Dogs and Cats" workshops demanded a text to ease their note-taking. My family and friends asked that it be very easy to understand and use. I hope all readers find it user-friendly.

My intent is to share information that I have derived from many sources, including educational courses, seminars, lectures, workshops, and study groups; researchers, healers, breeders, and other animal lovers; and personal experience with my own animals and those of my students. I understand completely how much you can love your animal friends and can desire to have them with you, happy and healthy, for as long as possible. As a result, I have fed my own cats and dogs the diet recommended in this book for over a decade, and I have raised multiple generations of healthy animals on it. If the information interests you, I encourage you to continue learning all that you can about animal nutrition. Nutritional education is ongoing, for we are learning new things every day about the miracle that is life, and about what it takes to sustain it in optimal health.

I suppose my interest in nutrition was predestined, as I came into the world with a hefty share of health problems. I muddled along well enough until a crippling muscle disorder in my legs grew worse as I got older. I spent many years going from one medical specialist to the next, until I had almost resigned myself to spending the rest of my life in a wheelchair borrowed from my grandmother, living on painkillers and antidepressants. I received an array of diagnoses, from multiple sclerosis to a mysterious neurological disorder. My dear husband began rearranging his life in order to best take care of me. Then, one wonderful day, a new acquaintance suggested that I make an appointment with her doctor, a nutritional pioneer with a holistic family practice. *Well,* I thought, *it's the one sort of doctor that I haven't seen yet, so I'll give it a try.* As remarkable as it may seem, the first day I met Dr. Richard Dahout was the last day that I ever used my wheelchair. The miracle "cure" was simply proper nutrition. Dr. Dahout taught me how to properly nourish my body with foods that I needed to enjoy good health.

If you put yourself in my place, you can imagine how this transformation affected me. It changed my life forever! I traded in my wheelchair and painkillers for control over my body through the foods I ate. It had been so long since I could walk without pain—now, suddenly, I was able to walk, and even run, whenever I wanted to! And since I am a totally-crazy-about-animals person, I became determined to learn how to feed my dogs and cats so that they too could enjoy a better quality of life. I knew that if food could make such a big difference in my health, it could also have a positive influence on their health. My life-saver became my first teacher, as Dr. Dahout generously shared his incredible nutritional knowledge with me. I believe that he appreciated my passion for animal nutrition because it paralleled his own for humans.

In addition to learning from Dr. Dahout, I traveled throughout the United States taking courses, classes, and workshops. I talked to people who successfully raised healthy animals and studied the diets of wild animals. My library outgrew my bookcases. Along the way, I earned certifications in clinical nutrition and in animal health instruction. As I started to apply this newfound knowledge to my animal companions, I was overwhelmed by the positive difference it made in their well-being. As their health increased, other animal lovers began to notice and ask questions. And so I began teaching and sharing what I had learned, and what I am still learning. To me, there is no greater reward for my effort than seeing dogs and cats enjoy the optimum quality of life that is their birthright.

This is the true joy of life,
. . . being used for a purpose recognized by yourself as a
mighty one;. . . being a force of nature instead of a feverish,
selfish, little clod of ailments and grievances complaining
that the world will not devote itself to making you happy.

I am of the opinion that my life belongs to the
whole community and as long as I live it is my
privilege to do for it whatever I can.

I want to be thoroughly used up when I die, for the harder
I work the more I live. I rejoice in life for its own sake.

Life is no 'brief candle' to me.
It is a sort of splendid torch which I have got hold of for the
moment, and I want to make it burn as brightly as possible
before handing it on to future generations.

— George Bernard Shaw

CHAPTER ONE

Species-Appropriate Nutrition

Each new day brings validity to what wise nutritionists—and your mother—have been saying for years: Eat good food and stop eating junk! Our own doctors encourage us to consume fewer processed foods and rely more on unadulterated natural ingredients in our meals if we wish to enjoy an optimal quality of life. Surely, our beloved animal companions are entitled to the same consideration.

Why does the quality of food make a difference in your pet's health? Simply put, food is body fuel, and life does not exist without it. The strength of your pet's immune system, its resistance to disease, and its quality of life all depend on the type and quality of food that it eats.

Although commercial pet food products may be extremely convenient, they lack vital enzymes and provide only a fixed formula, with no healthy variety of fresh foods. All ingredients are heated, making many of them less viable, and some of them actually dangerous, to health. Take a moment and ask yourself if you would eat these products. Would you feed them to your human children, day after day, year after year, for their entire lives? Probably not. Common sense and current knowledge have proven that we must eat a wide variety of fresh, wholesome foods to enjoy good health. The same wisdom applies to our pets.

Just as processed foods are a new addition to the human diet, they are also a recent substitution for unadulterated foods in the diets of our canine and feline friends. Until the invention of processed commercial pet food products—less than 100 years ago—all animal lovers shared their own food with their dogs and cats. In fact, people have been making their animal companions' meals at home since the beginning of our relationship with them, which was about 4,000 years ago for cats and 14,000 years ago for dogs. Many people all over the world have continued to prepare their furry friends' food at home.

A Dog, a Cat, a Koala

Each species on our planet has been shaped by eons of evolution to thrive in good health by eating specific foods. These food requirements vary with the physiology of each species, and every species must consume familiar foods to best fulfill their nutritional requirements. If all species were designed to eat the same foods, we'd soon be out of food! Obviously, our dogs and cats were not designed to eat eucalyptus leaves while swaying in the branches of a tall tree like the koala. Nor have they evolved to consume plankton, like many of the great whales, or to graze exclusively on plants like a cow or horse. Evolution has been designing our dogs' and cats' digestive systems for at least 120 million years.

According to their physiology, dogs and cats are carnivores. They have teeth and claws designed to catch, rip, and tear flesh. They have eyes in the front of their heads, enabling them to focus on prey animals (most of which have eyes on the sides of their head to watch for carnivorous attacks). Cats and dogs have short digestive systems, designed to digest food quickly. They are equipped with the digestive enzymes and other natural chemicals needed to digest the specific foods that they have evolved to eat.

Even with the many changes that humans have made to the exteriors of our domesticated dogs and cats, they still retain their original carnivorous features. In fact, in 1993 the American Society of Mammalogists' Mammal Species of the World, adhering to the Code of the International Commission on Zoological Nomenclature, officially designated the dog and the wolf as the same species, *Canis lupus.* When dogs and cats are allowed to become wild, or feral, it takes very few generations for them to resemble their wild relatives. Internally, they have never changed. The domesticated cat, *Felis catus,* is classified as belonging to the family of flesh-eating, predaceous mammals, including the lion, tiger, cougar, leopard, lynx, and others.

Domestication of the cat was advantageous to humans; due to their carnivorous nature, they helped to rid us of rodents and other "pests." In addition to their physiology, our dogs and cats also still retain many behavioral patterns of their wild relatives. And even though the dog may scavenge more than the cat, both were designed to thrive on a diet consisting mainly of other animals. But make no mistake, being a carnivore does not mean that our dogs and cats should eat an all-meat diet. Surely, we have never seen herds of pot roasts and hamburgers running through the forest. Carnivores such as our dogs and cats have evolved to derive their needed nutrients mainly from eating other animals, including those animals' muscle meat, bones, organs, and stomach contents—all raw.

Raw Food

Over a period of ten years, from 1932 to 1942, in a strictly controlled experiment involving 900 cats, Francis Pottenger Jr., M.D., proved the importance of feeding raw food to animals. The study was conducted within the most rigorous scientific standards of the day, and the pathological and chemical findings were also supervised by Alvin G. Foord, M.D., professor of pathology at the University of Southern California and pathologist at the Huntington Memorial Hospital in Pasadena.

Dr. Pottenger found a startling contrast in health between cats fed a cooked food diet and cats fed a raw food diet. The cats on the raw food diet thrived in good health. They reproduced easily, and their kittens were uniform in size and vigor. The cats that were fed cooked food swiftly deteriorated in health until, by the third generation, they could no longer reproduce. These cats suffered from behavior problems, allergies, skin problems, parasites, skeletal deformities, organ malfunctions (including those of the heart, thyroid, kidney, liver, testes, ovaries, and bladder), and inflammation of the nervous system.

When the first- and second-generation cooked-food cats were placed on a raw food diet, it took four generations for their line to recover from the ill effects of consuming cooked food. The study found that when a female cat was fed a cooked food diet even for only 12 to 18 months, she was unable to ever give birth to normal kittens. But, when her kittens were placed on a raw food diet, a gradual regeneration took place. Dr. Pottenger's theory proved true: that heat alters raw food, with a negative effect on health.

Biologists have yet to discover any wild carnivore that cooks its food. A carnivore's body has been designed to derive its needed nutrients from raw food. Many successful zoos and other captive habitats have discovered that they cannot keep their animals healthy and able to reproduce unless they are fed raw food. Cooking or heat processing actually changes the molecular structure of food, binding food molecules tighter together. This makes them more difficult to digest and transforms them into "foreign" or unfamiliar food.

Cooked food takes longer to digest and therefore requires more of the animal's energy. Heat also destroys enzymes and antioxidants, which are very important for good health. In fact, enzymes are needed for every biochemical activity in your dog's or cat's body. And, unfortunately, the body has a limited supply of its own enzymes. It is designed to consume enzymes in raw food. When the pancreas is called upon to produce enzymes because the ingested cooked food has none, the pancreas must enlarge and work harder than it is designed to. When stressed, the pancreas sends white blood cells, or leukocytes, to the digestive system to aid in digestion. But when the leukocytes use their enzymatic activity to aid digestion, they are less able to help destroy bacteria and foreign invaders in the body. This impairs the immune system.

There are many biochemical interactions that occur within the body, creating necessary nutrients such as some of the B vitamins and vitamin K. Cooked food interferes with many of these normal processes. Studies have found that when meat is cooked at high temperatures, cancer-forming compounds develop that interfere with the body's genetic structure. Heat also destroys many vital amino acids, vitamins, and minerals—some of which, undoubtedly, we have yet to even discover.

Cooking food also transforms its essential fatty acids, which are so named because they are essential to your pet's health. They must come from food sources. When essential fatty acids are heated or exposed to light or oxygen, they become trans-fats—dangerous toxins that weaken your pet. Research confirms that trans-fats have a detrimental effect on the reproductive system, immune system, cell membranes, cardiovascular system, and liver function. Trans-fats also do not provide good transport throughout the body for fat-soluble vitamins.

A Raw Diet Enhances Health

We can trace our dogs' and cats' ancestries back to a prehistoric carnivore that lived 120 million years ago. *Cynodictis,* predecessor to the dog, lived 40 million years ago (see the timeline that follows). The outside appearance of our dogs and cats may have been changed by human selection, but the inside of our furry friends is still that designed by evolution. The digestive design of your feline or canine companion is not changed simply because it's living in your condo! Your domesticated carnivore still needs species-appropriate nutrition to achieve optimum health.

The closer we can simulate the diet that evolution designed our dogs and cats to thrive on, the closer we will be to providing nutrients in the form that our animal companions need to enjoy good health. Since few of us are willing or able to provide whole prey animals for our pets to eat, making a well-designed homemade diet of raw foods is the next best thing.

A few of the benefits of feeding a species-appropriate diet of raw foods to your dog or cat include: stronger disease and parasite resistance, elimination of bad body odor and breath, healthy skin and coat, improved digestion, clean teeth, strong nails, healthy ears, and the satisfaction of knowing exactly what your pet is eating. By switching our pets to a well-prepared species-appropriate diet of raw foods, we may enable them to enjoy the optimum quality of life that they deserve.

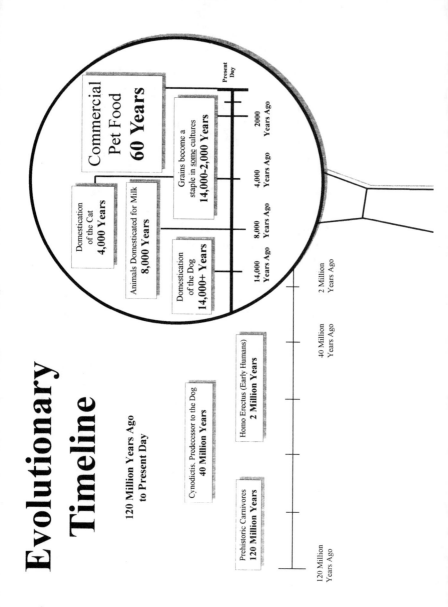

Evolutionary Timeline

120 Million Years Ago to Present Day

Prehistoric Carnivores
120 Million Years

Cynodictis, Predecessor to the Dog
40 Million Years

Homo Erectus (Early Humans)
2 Million Years

120 Million Years Ago

40 Million Years Ago

2 Million Years Ago

Domestication of the Dog
14,000+ Years

Animals Domesticated for Milk
8,000 Years

Domestication of the Cat
4,000 Years

Grains become a staple in some cultures
14,000–2,000 Years

Commercial Pet Food
60 Years

14,000 Years Ago

8,000 Years Ago

4,000 Years Ago

2000 Years Ago

Present Day

*"The greatness of a nation and its moral progress
can be judged by the way its animals are treated."*

— Gandhi

CHAPTER TWO

The Ultimate Diet

Ask ten different people what the best food for dogs and cats is, and you'll probably hear ten different answers. Companion-animal nutrition is a hotly debated topic, and opinions are often very personal and strongly felt. How we feed our animals is closely tied to our own personal philosophies. There is no "one" method of feeding animals that is correct for all owners. To be successful, a diet must make both animal and owner happy.

It is pointless to debate whether or not dogs and cats can be maintained in good health on home-prepared meals. People have been feeding their animal companions homemade meals since the beginning of the human/animal relationship, about 4,000 years ago for cats and 14,000 years ago for dogs. Actually, current theory places domestication of the dog at around 14,000 years ago, but a newer theory proposes 100,000 years. The newer theory is unconfirmed partly due to the fact that fossilized wolf and dog bones are difficult to differentiate.

In the evolutionary timeline, commercial animal diets have only been with us for a mere blink of time, about 60 or so years. Obviously, before their advent, people did manage to adequately feed their animals and keep them in excellent health on diets prepared at home. People have not suddenly become inept! Certainly, if you manage to feed yourself, and perhaps a family, too, you can manage to feed your dog or cat. It's not really much different. Actually, it's easier.

To help make feeding your pet as easy as it should be, there is a very important concept that you need to embrace. It is probably the most difficult part of preparing your pet's meal, because it requires you to change the way your bio-computer (your brain) may think. If you can teach yourself this lesson, you're well on your way to preparing easy, nutritious, stress-free meals for your dog or cat.

Clear your mind and take a deep breath. Ready? Here it is: Stop focusing on exact "percentages" of ingredients. Humans who have been feeding their pets from cans or bags have gotten used to feeding their pets "percentages" of nutrients. But we ourselves don't eat this way, and we don't feed our human children this way. You don't dine at a restaurant and order "22% protein, 10% fat, 25% fiber, and 40% moisture!" We don't prepare meals for our human families by using exact percentages of nutritional components to ensure a balanced diet. And, unless we are on a weight-loss diet, we rarely focus on exact amounts. We don't fix our dinner saying to ourselves, "I must have exactly 1.2 cups of turkey, 1 cup of mashed potatoes, .3 cup of gravy, 2 tablespoons of cranberry sauce, and .5 cup of vegetables."

There is no reason to feed your dog or cat this way either. Stop thinking in precise percentages and amounts of food for your pet. Remind yourself that you don't eat this way. Wild dogs and cats certainly don't eat this way either. Think "food groups" and "balance" instead. Yes, the general proportions of foods that you feed your pet are important. But don't torture yourself over it, because it's not that difficult to get right.

Remember, you do prepare good, healthy, homemade meals frequently for yourself (and perhaps growing children) without tormenting yourself over ingredients and amounts. You can do the same for your furry friend. Sure, the food might be in a form slightly different from what you would eat, but basically, think of preparing your pet's meal as preparing a normal homemade meal for a person. It doesn't need to be any more complicated. People have been feeding their healthy pets this way for centuries.

The easiest and most accurate method of balancing the correct proportions of food is to think "prey animal." Basically, you will build a prey animal for your domesticated carnivore. If you can't visualize it, visit a zoo, a pet store that sells small animals, or a butcher shop that stocks whole carcasses. Look closely at the birds, rabbits, mice, rats, and fish. Those are prey animals. Your dog or cat would love to have a look at them!

In the appendix, I will offer some guidelines of amounts of food to get you started, but please don't focus too much on adhering to exact amounts, because every animal is an individual. Amounts depend greatly on exercise, climate, temperament, growth, predispositions, and other factors—just like humans. In fact, one of the best things about feeding a homemade diet to your pet is that the ingredients are so flexible. You can prepare a meal that caters to your animal's individual needs. Just don't leave important ingredients out, and don't stray from that prey-animal balance of ingredients.

Keep in mind that a rabbit, bird, or mouse consists of lots of raw muscle meat, raw bone, some raw organ meat, a little predigested stomach content, and some extras. A wild dog or cat would also nibble on a few other foods in addition to the prey animal, including yummy insects, eggs, and plants, and we'll add these other nutrients as extras, treats, and snacks.

Basic Food Groups

Most people learned about the basic food groups in school. It is probably the most popular method of discerning the correct balance of food for human meals. Here are some basic food groups for your dog and cat:

1. Raw meat. In this group we have protein foods including beef, fish, poultry, lamb, and rabbit. This food group includes both muscle and organ meat. Muscle meat is the flesh located between the skin and bones of an animal. Organ meat includes the internal organs of the animal. Proportionately, you should feed more muscle meat than organ meat, and meat for most dogs and cats can have a high fat content. Frequent inclusion of a small portion of raw heart is good, especially for cats. According to many experts, whether or not a wild carnivore eats the organs and stomach contents of a prey animal depends on personal preference and pack status. Even though organ meat is rich in nutrients, too much can upset nutritional balance and cause a loose stool. Feed it in smaller amounts than the muscle meat.

You may also add whole raw eggs to the meat portion of your pet's meal a few times each week. Do not feed raw salmon unless it has tested free of salmon poisoning. Although some animal caretakers successfully feed raw pork, many animals find it difficult to digest. Feeding muscle meat in chunk form is best, but unfortunately this allows pets to shake off, or eat around, other important diet ingredients. By feeding muscle meat in ground or minced form, you will be able to thoroughly mix the other ingredients into the meal. Always feed meat that is fit for human consumption. If possible, buy organically fed, free-range meat.

If the possible bacteria content in raw meat alarms you, remember what species you are feeding it to. Dog's and cat's digestive systems have evolved over millions of years to get the nutrients necessary for good health from raw meat. Their digestive system is short and acidic, perfect for handling bacteria. And you know how much some of them relish something old and really gross! *Canis lupus* eats not only fresh prey, but also old buried meat that is teeming with bacteria.

Your dog or cat adequately defends itself against bacteria daily. Many types of bacteria can be found normally in your pet's digestive system. In fact, beneficial bacteria in your pet's gut help keep bad bacteria from becoming a problem. Salmonella, E. coli, and other bacteria are on many surfaces that your pet often comes into contact with. Salmonella has even been found in samples of commercial pet foods and treats. Bacteria is not a problem for a pet with a strong immune system, and a strong immune system is encouraged by eating species-appropriate raw food.

There is no evidence proving that the digestive systems of our domesticated dogs and cats are any weaker than that of their wild relatives. But there is much evidence indicating that raw meat promotes good health. And remember, not all types of bacteria are bad. Some types of bacteria are needed for healthy digestion.

If you prefer, you may add a good-quality antibacterial to your pet's meals. One such product is citrus seed extract. Do not use it full strength. Dilute it in the water that you use to mix the meal together with, per the directions on the bottle. You may soak chunks of meat and bones in it, too. You can also use it to kill bacteria in foreign water when you travel, and with pets that have been diagnosed with a weak or compromised immune system. If your pet suffers from yeast overgrowth or infections, using a good-quality citrus seed extract should help clear it up.

There are also other natural antibacterials. *Probiotics* are beneficial organisms that promote a healthy intestinal environment. They are widely available at health food stores. Tests show that non-dairy probiotics such as acidophilus/bifidus can be 97 percent effective in combatting E. coli bacteria. In fact, a course of non-dairy probiotics should be given to any animal that is taking antibiotics or has taken them in the past year. Alfalfa has proven effective against gram-negative bacteria (such as salmonella). Chamomile, garlic, kelp, ginger, and parsley are also antibacterial. Organic, raw, unfiltered apple cider vinegar kills some bacteria and contains many enzymes. You may give small dogs and cats 1 to 2 teaspoons, and larger pets 1 to 2 tablespoons, in their food. It is quite tart, so start with a small amount and gradually work up.

However, keep two things in mind: One is that your pet's digestive system has evolved over millions of years to thrive on raw meat, and two is that the best defense against disease is a strong immune system—which is built by consuming a species-appropriate diet of raw foods. One more very important point to remember regarding bacteria and germs, and please excuse the crudeness, but these are animals that lick their bottoms, after all!

By the way, eating raw meat in a homemade meal does not encourage your pet to kill animals, though this suggestion is often made. The instinct to chase and kill depends on your pet's individual prey drive and its early lessons from its mother or other animals. Your dog or cat does not connect the meat in its dish to a cow grazing in a pasture.

Raw meat, fish, and eggs provide the following species-appropriate array of nutrients—all in a form with high bioavailability:

- amino acids and protein
- enzymes
- antioxidants
- vitamins A, C, D, E, K, B_1, B_2, B_3, B_5, B_6, and B_{12}
- biotin
- choline
- folic acid
- inositol
- iodine
- pantothenic acid
- PABA
- fatty acids
- calcium
- phosphorus
- magnesium
- iron
- potassium
- chromium
- copper
- manganese
- selenium
- sodium
- sulfur
- vanadium
- zinc
- coenzyme Q_{10}

2. Raw bone. Our dogs and cats have relied on eating raw meaty bones as a superior source of nutrients for millions of years. Consider how much of a prey animal's body consists of raw bone—a lot. If you have a pet that hunts for itself, it's been consuming raw bones on its own, lucky pet! The most important thing to remember about this group is to *always* feed it raw. Cooking bone changes its molecular structure, making it splinter and difficult to digest. Cooked bone is very dangerous; please do not ever feed it.

On the other hand, raw edible bones offer wonderful nutrition in a form that is very natural and usable for your dog or cat. Not only do they offer a great nutrient profile, but raw meaty bones also supply good upper body and intestinal exercise. And, along with a proper body pH encouraged by eating raw food, they help keep teeth clean. Thousands of people all over the world, including many nutritionally oriented veterinarians, have found improved health for their dogs and cats by including raw, edible, meaty bones in their pets' diets.

Wild dogs and cats have always consumed raw bone, with great benefit. Raw meat and bones should constitute the majority of the feline or canine diet. Raw bones are different from bonemeal, which is a cooked and processed product, often high in lead content; it cannot match the nutrients found in raw, edible, meaty bones.

Edible bone is bone that your dog or cat can totally consume. Large raw-beef knuckle bones, for example, do offer some nutritional value and are great fun for pets, but are not totally consumed; therefore, not as many nutrients are derived from them. Raw poultry bones with a bit of meat on them are a great source of species-appropriate nutrition. Have you picked yourself up off the floor? Yes, poultry bones—but remember, *raw.* Raw poultry bones, such as chicken and turkey, are munched and crunched up quite easily. Remember the species of animal you are feeding; its entire digestive system is designed to eat raw meat and bones, including bird bones. If you have an outside cat that eats what it catches, it has been enjoying raw bones.

Although all parts of the bird may be fed, raw chicken necks are good to begin with for small dogs and cats. For larger dogs, raw chicken necks or backs, or turkey necks, will do nicely. Raw necks are full of good edible cartilage. You may have noticed that cartilage supplements for joint and bone problems now fill the shelves at veterinarians' offices, pet stores, and health food stores. Raw poultry necks are a less expensive and more natural form of these vital nutrients (and are a lot more fun for your pet!). Once you are accustomed to feeding raw necks, you may want to feed a variety of raw bones that includes backs, wings, legs, and other poultry parts. Chicken backs often come with organ meat attached, so you probably won't need to add other organ meat when feeding them. Large dogs may even enjoy an occasional meal consisting only of a whole chicken; small dogs and cats may like a smaller whole game bird.

Excluding raw meaty bones from your pet's diet would be a terrible mistake. Its diet would be extremely unbalanced and unhealthy without raw bone. For one thing, your pet would develop a calcium deficiency. Raw bone is a very species-appropriate source of calcium and many other important nutrients. In fact, raw meat and bones provide almost every nutrient your dog or cat needs to be healthy. Add a few other raw foods—including an occasional small portion of organ meat, vegetables, and some extras—and you've got a super meal for optimum health: the Ultimate Diet! And that optimum health includes mental health, because most dogs and cats love to eat bones. It makes them very happy. Many animal lovers call raw meaty bones "dog and cat candy"! Bones also firm up stools and help to naturally express the anal glands as Mom Nature intended.

When feeding necks, you'll notice that some raw chicken necks come with a lot of fat attached. Raw fat is good, but leaving it on all the necks may satiate your pet before enough other nutrients have been consumed—especially with a small or sedentary pet. In this case, just pull off the extra fat; the skin can be left on. If you have a large animal, especially one who burns a lot of calories, you may want to leave some of this fat on the neck, as it provides additional energy.

Since cats and dogs, unlike cows and horses, are not really built for chewing, they mostly just mash and crush bones before swallowing them. If they swallow a piece that is too big, they may bring it back up to continue crushing until it is smaller, and then swallow it again. This is normal, and pets that are new to bones usually become more adept as they gain experience.

If you are really having a difficult time with the concept of feeding your pet raw bones, remember that it is a very natural source of species-appropriate nutrients. Begin with raw chicken or turkey necks (depending on the size of your pet), as they are mostly cartilage and very flexible. You may also put them through a meat grinder or have your butcher grind them for you. Or you may wish to smash the necks with a mallet or hammer; pets that have many missing teeth may be fed their bones this way. If you grind or smash the bones, your pet will be missing out on some of the fun, exercise, and benefit of eating whole, raw, meaty bones, but at least it will still receive the good nutrition. Do not feed the homemade diet without some form of raw bone, or you will create nutritional deficiencies.

Raw, meaty bones provide nutritious marrow, amino acids/protein, essential fatty acids, fiber, enzymes, antioxidants, and a vast array of species-appropriate minerals and vitamins all in a usable form. Plus, they make pets happy!

3. Raw vegetables. This food group includes vegetables and plants that grow above and below the ground. Above-ground veggies include asparagus, broccoli, cabbage, cauliflower, celery, chard, dandelion greens, dark leaf lettuce, kale, okra, parsley, sprouts, squash, watercress, grasses, and so on. Fresh herbs may be included in this group. Use a good herbal reference book to ensure that any herbs you use are safe for your pet.

Vegetables that grow below-ground include potatoes—but do not feed green ones, or those with sprouted "eyes"—as well as sweet potatoes, yams, carrots, and the like. If you want to feed beets, do so only occasionally in very small amounts, and don't be alarmed if they come out the same color as they went in.

Fresh garlic is good in very small quantities. A small amount of fresh, organically grown ginger is an excellent addition to your veggie mix. It contains nutrients, and also has enzymatic and anti-inflammatory action.

To give your pet a variety of nutrients, feed a wide variety of vegetables, and combine a few different ones in each meal.

Include vegetables from both categories in every meal: that is, those that grow above and below the ground. For example, you might mix carrots, sweet potatoes, broccoli, parsley, and ginger. Do not feed only above- or below-ground veggies; feed both.

Don't give iceberg lettuce, as it has little nutritional value. Rhubarb and onions are best avoided, too. Sprouts should be fed only in moderation. Vegetables that are high in oxalic acid, such as spinach and chard, are good occasionally, but if fed every day may interfere with calcium absorption. Excess consumption of cruciferous vegetables (such as cabbage, broccoli, or kale) may interfere with thyroid function.

This should not be a problem if you simply remember to rotate a wide variety of veggies. Don't feed the same thing week after week. And don't feed veggies in excess. Remember that prey animal you're building? It probably has a pretty small stomach, and that's where your dog or cat would find most of its vegetable matter. As important as they are, don't go overboard with the veggies. Too many above-ground vegetables can loosen stools and upset pH balance. Keep in mind that you're not feeding an herbivore.

For our dogs and cats to best utilize them, vegetables must be put into a digestible form, just as they would be in a prey animal's stomach. Use a food processor, blender, or juicer to thoroughly pulp vegetables before feeding, and feel free to use veggie parts that might otherwise be thrown away, such as broccoli stems and celery and carrot tops.

Raw vegetables provide the following nutrients. Organically grown vegetables offer the most nutritional value.

- en
- a
-
-
-

- inosi
- iodine
- PABA
- pantothenic acid

- calcium
- chromium
- copper
- iron
- iodine
- magnesium
- manganese
- molybdenum
- phosphorus
- potassium
- silicon
- sodium
- sulfur
- selenium

4. Extras. This group helps make up for the lower nutrient content of modern foods, caused in part by soil depletion or similar factors. In addition, extras help supply nutrients found in a wild diet, as well as ones that help our pets cope with environmental toxins and other stresses of our modern world. If your pet has a digestive disorder, it is a good idea to also add a digestive enzyme and a non-dairy probiotic to its meal. The basic extras include:

Kelp and alfalfa. A combination of these two green foods is a powerful addition to the Ultimate Diet, due to their impressive nutrient and medicinal value. Alfalfa contains vitamins A, B_1, B_3, B_5, B_6, B_{12}, C, D, E, K, and U, plus beta-carotene, biotin, folic acid, calcium, phosphorus, potassium, magnesium, iron, zinc, copper, protein, trace elements, and fiber. It has antibiotic action against gram-negative bacteria, such as salmonella. It also contains a protein with anti-tumor activity and reduces tissue damage from radiotherapy. Alfalfa is often used as a general tonic, to detoxify the body, and to treat colon and bleeding disorders, diabetes, ulcers, and arthritis.

Kelp contains vitamins A, B_1, B_3, B_5, B_6, B_9, B_{12}, C, and E, plus zinc, biotin, bromine, calcium, choline, copper, inositol, iodine, PABA, potassium, selenium, sodium, sulfur, trace elements, and fiber. Its iodine content is very good for glands and organs, especially the thyroid and liver. Kelp is also used for hair loss, goiter, obesity, arthritis, heart and circulatory disorders, mineral deficiency, and as a general tonic. It has anti-cancer, anti-rheumatic, and anti-inflammatory properties. Kelp has antibiotic action against gram-negative and -positive bacteria. As dietary fiber, both kelp and alfalfa help bind and neutralize carcinogens in the body. They are also helpful with radiation toxicity.

Quality is extremely important. Use fit-for-human-consumption, organically grown alfalfa, as it is cleaner and more nutrient-dense. Alfalfa's very deep root system bypasses many surface soil pollutants. Kelp should come from a clean, cold, deep ocean source. For best assimilation, use both in finely powdered form, mix 50/50 in an airtight glass jar, and store in a dark cupboard. Equal parts of powdered alfalfa and kelp in your pet's food provides a vast array of health-enhancing nutrients and acts as a complete vitamin and mineral supplement. This powerful combination need only be given in small quantity in proportion to the other diet ingredients.

If desired, you may also use other nutritional herbs or green foods that are seasonal or specifically helpful to your animal's condition by mixing them into the kelp/alfalfa blend. This will be discussed further in chapter 6.

Essential fatty acids. Every living cell in your dog's or cat's body needs essential fatty acids (EFAs), which help support healthy skin, hair, joints, and hearts. They are found in high concentrations in the brain. EFAs must be fed raw and unheated. Heat, light, and oxygen turn them into trans-fatty acids, which are very dangerous to health. Studies have proven that trans-fatty acids are toxins that weaken the immune system, reproductive system, cardiovascular system, and liver function, and that they also inhibit enzymes and contribute to free-radical formation.

Good food sources of EFAs include fish, fish oil, poultry, vegetable oils, dark green vegetables, eggs, raw nuts, and seeds. Flaxseed oil, hemp seed oil, fish body oil, and eggs from properly fed chickens offer a good supply of the important omega-3 fatty acids. For most pets, the most utilizable source of supplemental omega-3 fatty acids is a very high-quality fish body oil, but most pets can also use flaxseed oil. Hemp seed and flaxseed oils, like most vegetable oils, also contain omega-6 essential fatty acids.

If you have a cat or a hypothyroid dog, animal source EFAs may be utilized better than vegetable oil source EFAs. Opinions vary as to the correct ratio of EFAs for pets. The optimum supplemental amount of omega-3 and omega-6 your pet needs depends greatly on how much is in the raw food that it consumes. Raw meat provides your pet with both EFAs, with more omega-6 than omega-3. Grass-fed or wild meat animals contain more EFAs, especially omega-3, than grain-fed livestock. Eggs from free-range chickens also have a higher omega-3 content than eggs from caged hens. A pet who consumes lots of fresh fish will be getting more omega-3 EFAs than a pet who does not consume fish.

Generally, the more animal fat consumed (and utilized), the less supplemental omega-6 needed. Flaxseed oil provides both omega EFAs, with a higher ratio of omega-3. Hemp seed oil contains a balance of omega-3 and omega-6. Fish body oil provides a very usable source of omega-3. Organic, unheated safflower oil is high in omega-6.

Oils must be of very good quality and treated and stored with care. Buy organically grown oil that is unrefined and is processed without chemical solvents. Check expiration dates. Oils should never be heat-treated or taste bitter or rancid. They should come in dark bottles to keep out light. Fish oil should be unheated and from deep-sea, cold-water fish, and should be tested for quality, purity, toxins, and heavy metals. While fish body and vegetable oils are given for their omega-3 and omega-6 content, cod-liver oil is given for its unique EFAs and vitamins A and D. Because vitamins A and D are fat-soluble vitamins, cod-liver oil should not be given in large quantities. Store oils in your refrigerator, and shake them very gently before using. Do not leave the bottle open or at room temperature any longer than necessary.

Fats are the best source of species-appropriate energy (body fuel) and are used like carbohydrates by dogs and cats. Cancer cells can grow and multiply utilizing energy from actual carbohydrates, but they cannot utilize the energy derived from fats. Raw meat contains useful fat, and the fattiest cuts of meat are good for most dogs and cats, unless they have a liver or pancreas impairment.

Vitamin C. Dogs and cats do make vitamin C within their bodies. But with the level of toxins, pollution, and stress that they are inundated with in today's modern world, we can help strengthen their bodies by boosting their supply of C. This vitamin strengthens the immune system and supports collagen; it is anti-inflammatory, an antioxidant, and an antihistamine. Vitamin C is found in raw foods such as fruits, vegetables, and organ meats.

For large doses, use vitamin C in a buffered, powdered form such as calcium or sodium ascorbate. Calcium ascorbate is good for most pets, but due to its bitter taste, you'll need to begin with low doses and work up gradually. Sodium ascorbate is the most mild tasting, but may contribute to alkalinity when used in large doses over an extended period of time in sensitive animals. Vitamin C in the form of pure ascorbic acid is very acidic and may cause stomach upset in large amounts. Besides, it's very sour, and not all animals, especially cats, enjoy the taste.

The best vitamin C supplement is one made from a natural source including bioflavonoid co-factors. Purchase vitamin C without fillers and sweeteners. Giving it in powdered form aids assimilation. One way to give your pet exactly the amount of vitamin C that it needs is by using it to "bowel tolerance." This works very well when you have a stressed animal that needs all the C it can use. Vitamin C is a water-soluble vitamin, and an excess will cause a loose stool. To use it to bowel tolerance, you begin with a low dose and increase the amount slightly every other day until you create a loose stool. Then, return to the previous dose that did not create a loose stool. This is how much your pet needs at this time. Very young pups and kittens can be given a liquid pediatric formula. Start with the lowest dose and work up gradually. Do not abruptly stop giving vitamin C. If you wish to reduce the dose, lower it gradually.

The diet discussed above—a well-prepared, homemade, species-appropriate meal of raw food—provides your furry friend with a wide array of usable nutrients, including:

- amino acids/protein
- antioxidants
- carbohydrates
- essential fatty acids
- enzymes
- fiber
- phytochemicals
- vitamins A, B_1, B_2, B_3, B_5, B_6, B_{12}, B_{13}, B_{15}, C, D, E, F, K, P, T, and U
- beta-carotene
- bioflavonoids
- biotin
- boron
- calcium
- choline
- chromium
- chlorine
- cobalt
- coenzyme Q_{10}
- copper
- fluorine

- folic acid
- germanium
- iodine
- inositol
- iron
- magnesium
- manganese
- molybdenum
- PABA
- pantothenic acid
- phosphorus
- potassium
- selenium
- silica
- sodium
- sulfur
- vanadium
- zinc
- the many other important nutrients for optimum health that we have yet to label

All these nutrients can be supplied by the Ultimate Diet, which can be graphically summed up by the following Raw Food Pyramid. To conclude the chapter, consider the Diet Comparison chart, which sums up some of the reasons that many animal guardians feed a raw food diet.

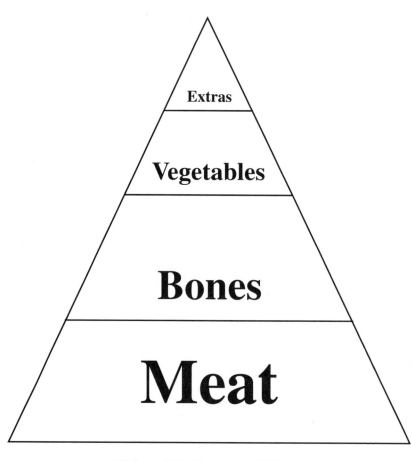

**The Ultimate Diet
Raw Food Pyramid**

DIET COMPARISON

The Ultimate Diet

Raw Meat
Contains: undamaged amino acids/protein, fat, antioxidants, enzymes, essential fatty acids, vitamins, and minerals.

Raw Bone
Contains: undamaged amino acids/protein, fat, fiber, antioxidants, enzymes, essential fatty acids, vitamins, and minerals.

Raw Vegetables
Contains: undamaged vitamins, minerals, carbohydrates, fiber, enzymes, essential fatty acids, phytochemicals, and antioxidants.

Essential Fatty Acids
Contains: undamaged omega 3 and 6, vitamins, and trace elements.

Kelp/Alfalfa
Contains: undamaged protein, carbohydrates, vitamins, minerals, phytochemicals, trace elements, antioxidants, and fiber.

Processed Pet Food Product

Cooked Meat
Contains: altered amino acids/protein, altered vitamins and minerals. Questionable bioavailability. Trans-fats. *No* enzymes or antioxidants.

Bonemeal
Contains: possible high contaminant and lead content. Altered protein, altered vitamins and minerals. *No* enzymes or antioxidants.

Grain
Contains: refined carbohydrates with altered nutrients. May contain mold, fungus, aflatoxins, and phytic acid, which may inhibit nutrient absorption. *No* enzymes or antioxidants. *No* nutritional need in cats and dogs. See chapter 7, "Foods to Avoid."

Vitamins and Minerals
May expire before use. Amount may be over or under recommendations. May have low bioavailability.

Fiber
May contain beet pulp, wood pulp, newspaper, or peanut shells.

The Ultimate Diet, cont'd.

Vitamin C
Contains: viable vitamin C for a strong immune system and optimum health.

Processed Pet Food Product, cont'd.

Denaturing Chemicals
Used to keep pet foods out of the human food chain, making them "not fit for human consumption."

Artificial Preservatives, Dyes, Flavorings
Many have been linked to cancer, epilepsy, birth defects, liver and kidney problems, allergies, behavioral disorders, reproductive problems, cataracts, and other health disorders.

*"To create health,
you need a new kind of knowledge,
based on a deeper concept of life."*

— Deepak Chopra, M.D.

❧ ❧ ❧

CHAPTER•THREE

Making the Meal

A nything new requires time and repetition to become a habit. Preparing your pet's new meal may seem awkward at first, but once it becomes a habit, it will be quite easy. Be patient and give yourself time to become accustomed to something new. Make a few copies of the Menu Sheet in the appendix, fill one out, and post it where you can see it in the feeding area. At first, you'll need to look at it often to remember all the ingredients. Eventually, you'll know it by heart, and preparation time will be minimal.

To actually put the meal together is very simple. Get out all your ingredients. Don't step on your dog or cat who has eagerly entwined itself around your legs in anticipation of something yummy! Put the veggies through the blender, processor, or juicer until they're pulpy. Measure them after pulping.

Put them in your pet's dish, along with the meat and extras. Add enough warm water to take the chill off food from the refrigerator. You want to serve food as close to room temperature as possible. Cold food may cause stomach discomfort and takes longer to digest. However, don't pour hot water directly onto oils, as they're very fragile. Pour the water to the side of the ingredients, then mix and serve. Make the food mushy, but not soupy.

You can feed the bones two ways: mixed with the rest of the meal, or fed as dessert. For most pets, the meaty bones are definitely their favorite part of the meal. For this reason, most people feed them as dessert and maintain the rule that "you don't get dessert until you've finished your dinner." Briefly rinse cold meaty bones in hot water to bring them to room temperature before feeding. Do not encourage heavy exercise after eating. If your pets initiate play among themselves, fine, but do not initiate exercise for them.

Food and Water Dishes

Feed and water your dog or cat in lead-free ceramic, glass, or stainless steel dishes. If you have a favorite dish that you are not sure of, you can purchase an inexpensive lead-testing kit. Cracked ceramic dishes need to be replaced. Do not use plastic or aluminum. Plastic gives off toxic fumes, and it is also scraped off by your pet's teeth; plastic and its fumes are not part of any diet! Feed pets in their own individual dishes so you know exactly what they're eating. Separate dishes also help to avoid political problems within multiple-pet households.

Water Is Essential

Good quality water is essential to your pet's health and should be available at all times. Don't use tap water, and if you have well water, don't assume that it is any better. Tap water may contain many undesirable toxins, while well water may contain soil contaminants and an unbalanced mineral profile. Distilled or reverse osmosis water is best.

You may notice that when your dog or cat is eating a species-appropriate diet, it drinks less water. This is normal. Raw food contains a lot of moisture and is a natural source of liquid for your pet.

Why Buy Organic?

If you are able to purchase organically grown food, please do so. Organically grown food is higher in nutrient content and has not been treated with dangerous chemicals. For example, organically grown kale may contain up to twice the vitamin C content as non-organically grown kale. Commercially grown potatoes are often treated with a sprout-inhibiting chemical so they last longer in the store. These chemicals aren't a concern if you buy organically grown spuds.

If you cannot obtain organically grown produce, be certain to wash it thoroughly before including it in your pet's meal. Also, avoid irradiated and genetically engineered food. Free-range, organically fed meat animals are usually treated more humanely and have not been subjected to drugs that your pet doesn't need to eat.

When commercial ranchers use feed that includes meat by-products, litter, and other waste, it affects the quality of the meat that your pet eats. Supporting meat ranchers that strive to raise animals in a clean, healthy, humane environment including vegetarian drug-free feed is beneficial to both pets and people.

Free-range, organically fed chickens produce eggs higher in nutrient content than non-organically raised hens. When you include eggs in your dog's or cat's meal, you may include the shell if you are sure that it hasn't been coated with a preservative. Many commercially grown eggs are treated with a preservative to extend shelf life. Check your sources. If you are unsure, feed the egg and throw the shell away. If the shell has not been treated, you may feed it, too.

If you do not have access to organic foods in your area, feeding raw food that is "fit for human consumption" will still greatly benefit your pet's health. And perhaps if you create a demand for organic food, it will come to your area. Supporting organic farming has far-reaching, positive effects. It keeps chemicals out of our soil, water, and pet dishes. When you buy organically grown food, you are supporting an industry that is less damaging to the earth and to the health of your furry friends.

Resources for Diet Ingredients

Locating good-quality ingredients for your pet's meals may open up a whole new shopping experience for you! For meat and bones, check out health food stores, grocery stores, wholesalers, butchers, ethnic markets, local farmers, slaughterhouses, and 4-H clubs. If you live in the country, look for a ranch or farm that raises animals humanely and free of drugs. Talk with ranchers about buying animals who die of natural causes. Get to know your local meat manager or butcher. A smart meat manager knows that when you come to the store to buy meat, you'll probably buy other groceries as well. Your business is good for his or her business.

Don't buy meat that is labeled as "pet food" and not fit for human consumption. Buying in bulk and freezing extra usually reduces the price; this is an option, although frozen is not quite as good as fresh. An extra freezer placed in the garage is very useful. Many ingredients of the diet are not human favorites, so prices are often quite reasonable.

Produce can be found at health food stores, grocery stores, farmer's markets, and local growers. Try to use produce fresh daily without freezing or previous preparation. Organically grown food and free-range meats are best, but even commercially raised food will offer good nutrition for your pet. Wash produce thoroughly before using.

Good quality oils can be obtained at health food stores. Vitamin C is available through health food stores and by mail. Kelp and alfalfa can be purchased at health food stores, herb stores, and through many mail order companies. Buying in bulk from an herb company is usually much less expensive than buying at a local store.

The overall cost of feeding a homemade diet is kept to a minimum with judicious shopping. Shop sales, and use food that is not as popular with humans—fatty meats and produce parts that are usually discarded. Carrot and celery tops, and broccoli, cauliflower, and lettuce stems have good nutrition-al value. Once accustomed to the diet, most pets eat far less raw food than commercial food. Plus, the usual reduction in veterinarian bills helps, too!

"It is one of the miracles of science and hygiene that the germs that used to be in our food have been replaced by poisons."

— Wendell Berry

ॐ ॐ ॐ

CHAPTER·FOUR

How Often Should Your Pets Eat?

Generally speaking, normal, non-pregnant, non-lactating adult dogs and cats over one year of age should eat one meal per day, six days per week. One day per week is a fast day. The homemade diet provides a great nutrient profile, so eating once a day will satisfy your pets' needs once they are accustomed to it. Carnivores are not grazing animals who should eat continually throughout the day. Digestion requires a lot of the body's energy, and an adequate break between meals is necessary to use that energy for healing and other body functions. Never leave food available all day, with one exception: a big raw knuckle bone occasionally for gnawing pleasure.

Young pups and kittens are fed two to four times daily; by one year of age, those meals should be gradually combined into one. Young giant-breed dogs may occasionally need an extra snack during growth spurts. Animals with diagnosed blood-sugar disorders may do better at first on two meals a day. If their problem resolves itself on the new diet, you may try reducing them to one meal daily.

Feeding once per day may be a new idea to people who have breeds believed to be prone to bloat. But research has found that dogs who eat table scraps and homemade food are less likely to bloat than dogs eating a commercial food only. Problems may be possible when combining raw foods with inappropriate foods, such as processed foods and the foods cautioned against in this book. On the Ultimate Diet, my deep-chested big dogs have never experienced bloat. It is your responsibility as your pet's guardian to do what you believe is best. An inquisitive mind and the desire for further education will help guide you.

An option you may incorporate into your feeding program is to feed the complete meal four or five days per week, feed a meal of meaty bones (bones with ample meat) only (or a whole chicken for large dogs, a game hen for smaller dogs and cats) one or two days per week, and fast one day per week. Otherwise, feed the four-food-group meal six days per week with one fast day.

Fasting

Dogs and cats over one year of age should fast, or rest their digestive system, one day per week. Dogs and cats under one year of age may fast half a day once per week. If animals are ill, they should fast under the supervision of an experienced veterinary practitioner. Fasting is a normal occurrence for wild carnivores. It enables the energy used for digestion to be used elsewhere in the body. For this reason, many dogs and cats instinctively fast when ill. Even when an animal is not ill, fasting encourages the body to heal and cleanse itself.

If you have a very difficult time putting your animal on a fast, a large raw knuckle bone only may be given one day per week. But, since this is not truly fasting, try to work toward a real fast day. Always provide lots of clean, good-quality drinking water for your pet. This is especially important on fast day, when the water will help flush toxins out of the body. If your pet reminds you of dinnertime on fast day, just be sure to offer attention and affection in a confident manner. Feeding your pet gives them attention, so on fast day, don't neglect this interaction. Play, train, or just give extra pats, and let them know that they are loved and that you will fix them a fabulous meal tomorrow.

"Come forth into the light of things,
let Nature be your teacher."

— William Wordsworth

Ỵ Ỵ Ỵ

CHAPTER • FIVE

Snacks, Treats, and Travel

Food is love, and we love to give our pets special tidbits for rewards or in training. Many commercial treats have unhealthy ingredients, so read labels carefully. Fortunately, there are healthy foods that we can use, including raw nuts and seeds. Always use raw, unsalted nuts and seeds only. Nuts and seeds are very high in fat, which can easily become rancid with heat. Raw seeds are especially nutritious when sprouted. Don't give your pet peanuts or peanut products, as they may contain aflatoxin, a dangerous carcinogen. Also, do not give them alfalfa seeds. After you open a package of raw nuts or seeds, seal and store it in the refrigerator. Fruit is another tasty treat for your dog or cat; it is high in natural sugar and moisture and is digested very quickly. It should always be fed at least a half hour away from other foods, or it may speed them through the digestive system too quickly and cause stomach upset. Too much fruit will cause a loose stool. Dried fruit can be used occasionally, but make sure it is unsulfured and not treated with chemicals. All fruit should be fed in moderation.

Large (too big to swallow) raw-beef knuckle bones can offer hours of gnawing pleasure. If your pet gets loose stools from the big hunks of pure beef fat on some knuckle bones, simply trim some of it off before serving next time. Whole vegetables such as carrots and broccoli stems may also be given, but since they are whole vegetables, don't be surprised if they come out of your pet in chunks. In their whole form, they are mainly for fun and fiber. Avoid rawhide and plastic bones, pig ears, and similar "treats." Most of these are treated with many unhealthy chemicals and contain rancid fat.

The treats and snacks mentioned above provide many good nutrients for your cat or dog. If you do not give raw nuts and seeds separately, then at mealtime you should occasionally toss a few into the food processor with the veggies. If your pet is not a fruit fan, try different varieties. And don't forget to occasionally offer a large raw-beef knuckle bone for good gnawing and nutrition. If you have a kind and brave butcher, you can have them saw a very large knuckle or femur bone in half lengthwise to make the yummy marrow more available to your furry friend.

Traveling with Your Pet

Yes, you can travel with the Ultimate Diet. There are a couple different methods you may use; both require that you bring an ice chest with ice or cold packs. One way to travel with the diet is to prepare complete meals in advance and store them in containers within the ice chest. Another way is to use "finger foods" only. You bring, or buy at local stores while traveling, whole foods that require little preparation. This would include whole raw bones with ample meat on them, lightly steamed or baked vegetables (since you're not pulping), and sugar-free, chewable vitamin C tablets. Because this method doesn't include all the extras, use for short trips only.

"The Lord hath created medicines out of the earth;
and he that is wise will not abhor them."

— Apocrypha, Ecclesiasticus 34:4

CHAPTER • SIX

Herbs and Green Foods

Herbs are simply plants, some of which you're already familiar with. That sprig of parsley garnishing your dinner plate was originally served with meals to aid digestion and cleanse the breath. The use of herbs in health care is as old as we are, documented in Roman, Egyptian, Persian, and Hebrew history. Herbs are also the foundation of our modern pharmaceutical industry. Many drugs have active elements originally isolated from herbs, such as digitalis from foxglove and atropine from belladonna.

Herbs are used medicinally and nutritionally because they are a concentrated source of nutrients and active compounds in an easily assimilated form. Herbs are effective because they contain many specific molecular principles in their natural state that have a wide variety of influences on the body.

Animals are natural herbalists, and wild animals instinctively use herbs for healing and nutritional value. Because we have much recorded information about herbs, we are able to choose those that are safe and that benefit our pet's well-being. Herbs should always be of good quality, given in fine powdered or liquid form, and stored in an airtight container away from moisture and sunlight. With the increased popularity of herbal medicine, many wild herbs are being overharvested and threatened with extinction. Choose herbs that are organically grown and not wild-harvested.

Herbs can be very deep, but slow, healers within the body. You may need more patience when treating a health problem with herbs instead of drugs, because healing the underlying cause of a problem often takes longer than just suppressing the symptoms.

A combination of powdered alfalfa and kelp is an important part of the Ultimate Diet. Mixing equal parts of these two foods results in a superb vitamin and mineral supplement; the benefits that these foods offer are discussed in chapter 2.

Although not an essential part of the diet, there are many other herbs and green foods that can be used for their nutritional and/or medicinal value, according to your individual animal's specific needs, including the following:

- Aloe vera is used both internally and externally for its soothing qualities.
- Cayenne is used for the circulatory and respiratory systems.
- Dandelion greens are rich in potassium and aid the liver.
- Garlic has a long history of use against parasites, bacteria, and fungus.
- Ginger is a potent antioxidant, anti-inflammatory, and digestive aid.
- Milk thistle is very popular for liver function.

- Nettles are very nutritious.
- Parsley is high in protein and is antibacterial.
- Peppermint is excellent for digestion.
- Rosemary is high in antioxidants and good for the heart and nerves.
- Slippery elm bark is soothing to mucous membranes.
- Wheatgrass, barley grass, and algae (chlorella, spirulina, or blue-green) provide chlorophyll and many nutrients.

Because the above are plants, they should be fed to carnivores in fairly small amounts, proportionately. Check with an animal herbal reference book before using, and always purchase good-quality products. Most dogs and cats enjoy nibbling on fresh grass and herbs, especially new spring growth. The vegetation that isn't completely digested acts as an internal cleanser; just be certain the plant has not been sprayed with chemicals. Indoor animals may enjoy nibbling on edible potted plants. Many are easy to grow in a sunny indoor spot.

Many herbs promote health, and most are safe enough to use confidently and effectively, but some require professional guidance. The best strategy is to research herbs one at a time before deciding whether to use them. There are many excellent reference books, including *The Scientific Validation of Herbal Medicine,* by Daniel B. Mowrey, Ph.D.; and *Herbal Remedies for Dogs and Cats,* by Mary Wulff-Tilford and Gregory L. Tilford.

*"For every disease that afflicts
mankind,there is a treatment or a cure
occurring naturally on the earth."*

— Dr. Norman Fansworth, pharmacoginist

ళ ళ ళ

CHAPTER SEVEN

Foods to Avoid

In 1997, oncologists from Colorado State University's College of Veterinary Medicine published diet recommendations to help combat the number-one killer of our beloved pets: cancer. Their recommendations suggest excluding lactate- and glucose-containing fluids, because cancer cells thrive on sugars and create lactate as a waste product. Lactate poisons the animal by depleting its energy, thus weakening it. The study recommends limiting sugars and simple carbohydrates. The researchers concluded that a diet relatively high in fat and low in simple carbohydrates resulted in a longer survival time for cancer victims.

Of note is the fact that cancer cells cannot utilize fat, which is an excellent natural energy source for dogs and cats. They also found that omega-3 fatty acids reduce lactate levels and have the ability to reduce or eliminate metastatic disease. Since heat and hydrogenation destroy these essential fatty acids, raw foods are a good source of these vital nutrients.

Sugar comes in many forms. Many processed and even "natural" foods contain sugar. Grains and dairy products are biologically inappropriate sources of sugar for dogs and cats.

The study also recommends feeding protein that is highly biodegradable. The body cannot utilize nutrients if it can't easily break down the food within the body.

A homemade species-appropriate diet can fulfill anti-cancer recommendations and may play a crucial role in prevention and treatment of this terrible disease. The above study only adds to the growing body of knowledge about many foods important to avoid, such as:

1. Sugar. As just discussed, cancer cells thrive on sugars. Sugar comes in many forms, including beet, raw, brown, cane, fructose, corn sweetener, corn syrup, date, dextrin, dextrose, glucose, lactose, maltose, manitol, polydextrose, sorbital, sorghum, sucanat, sucrose, turbinado, barley malt, molasses, honey, and maple syrup. Sugar is addictive, damages the pancreas, and drains vitamins and minerals from the body. It is implicated in hypoglycemia, diabetes, obesity, behavior problems, cataracts, tooth decay, arthritis, allergies, and cancer. Yeast also thrives on sugar. In a 1993 study, unhealthy candida yeast overgrowth was 200 times greater in animals receiving dextrose than in control groups that did not receive the sugar.

2. Chocolate. We've probably all heard that dogs and cats should not eat chocolate. It contains theobromine, which is a toxin for our furry friends, as well as caffeine, a nerve irritant. It also contains sugar.

3. Dairy products. Dairy products include milk, cream, butter, cheese, cottage cheese, yogurt, whey, sour cream, kefir, and ice cream. Milk is a hormonal growth fluid produced by a mother animal to nourish a youngster of her own species. Only rarely would a wild carnivore catch and eat a lactating prey animal or a just-fed newborn. Even so, this meal would contain little milk and in a form different from what is available commercially. The more natural forms, such as raw unpasteurized mouse milk or rabbit milk, are pretty difficult to come by in the market! And birds, a popular prey animal, don't nurse their young at all.

Humans are the only animals that choose to consume milk after weaning. Other animals, including wild cats and dogs, do not. Milk, and products made from milk, contain foreign hormones and lactose, a sugar. Most dogs and cats are not equipped with the lactase enzyme needed to digest lactose. Milk is also mucus-forming. Calcium is easily obtained from much more species-appropriate sources such as raw bones.

4. Grain. Dogs and cats have no nutritional need for grains. Carbohydrates or energy from grains is not required by dogs and cats. Fats are their best, species-appropriate source of energy, and they are also able to derive energy needs from protein. Energy is the "fuel" that sustains life and all bodily functions.

Wild prey animal stomachs may contain grasses, bark, insects, roots, nuts, seeds, and other plant matter—but not modern grain, unless the animal was grazing previously in a field of domesticated grain. Even so, the majority of our dogs' and cats' evolutionary history, which formed their physiology, did not include prey animals that ate domesticated grain. Grains were domesticated and used as a staple in some human cultures only recently in evolutionary history, so prey animals and predators did not have access to them until that time. And domesticated grains differ structurally from wild grains. Everything about our dogs' and cats' anatomy dictates that they are not natural grain eaters.

Grains break down into sugar within the body and can supply nourishment for yeast overgrowth. Grains are also mucus-forming and may contribute to many health problems including allergies, ear infections, skin problems, bloating, joint problems, malabsorption, and digestive disorders. Dr. Russell Swift, a nutritionally oriented veterinarian, feels that feeding grains to carnivores weakens their immune system and pancreas and may also lead to dental calculus. For cats and dogs, a good source of energy within a truly natural diet can be secured with raw fat and protein, not unnatural grain carbohydrates.

5. Raw salmon. Salmon poisoning is an infectious disease caused by a rickettsia that uses a parasite fluke on salmon as a host. It is mainly found in Pacific salmon, but any suspect fish may be tested. Avoid this danger by knowing the quality of the fish you are feeding to your pets.

6. Yeast. A very reliable remedy to rid your property of pesky ants is to mix yeast with sugar. The ants eagerly eat the mixture, which then expands, causing them to bloat, or explode, and die. Commercial yeasts are not natural foods for dogs and cats, and do not offer any nutrients that cannot be obtained from more species-appropriate sources. Yeast is a fungus, and most pets cannot tolerate it. Consuming yeast may also encourage yeast overgrowth within the body, which can lead to many health problems, including those of the digestive and urinary systems. Feeding yeast can unbalance your pet's calcium/phosphorus ratio due to yeast's high phosphorus content. Different forms of yeast include brewer's, nutritional, baker's, torula, and primary.

How to Improve Health

A well-prepared diet of raw meat, bones, vegetables, and extras provides a great nutrient profile of protein, essential fatty acids, vitamins, minerals, enzymes, antioxidants, and other health-enhancing nutrients in a form that evolution has designed our dogs and cats to easily utilize for optimal health and healing. When humans need to improve health, doctors recommend eating more fresh foods and fewer processed foods. The same biochemical logic applies to all animals.

Good nutrition is the foundation of health, but it is not a "magic bullet" that will enable your pet to live beyond its genetic potential. However, we can nourish those genes and give them the nutrients they require to function at their best by feeding foods that are biologically familiar and easily utilized. And we can encourage those genes to be healthier for the next generation. Dr. Bruce Cauble puts it very well when he writes, "You need only look at the digestive system of an organism to determine its appropriate diet."

A species-appropriate diet of raw foods has allowed many pets to overcome slight to debilitating health disorders.

And many pet guardians have been overjoyed to find that a good diet allows their dog or cat to enjoy an optimal quality of life. Good food provides the tools for building good health. However, there are other very important factors that should be considered in your pet's overall well-being, including physical and mental stress, environmental toxins, vaccinations, and radiation. Your own emotions and stress level also affect your pet's health. And don't neglect the importance of healthy exercise and a safe amount of daily sunlight (not through a window). As Dr. Stephen Blake says, regarding the diet outlined in this book, ". . . it provides an excellent foundation for building a healthier immune system to help your animals deal with the stresses of a polluted world." We have many choices to make regarding our pet's health. With an open mind, learn all that you can so you can make choices that both you and your furry friend can live with.

"The doctor of the future will give no medicines, but will interest his patients in the care of the human frame, in diet, and in the causes of disease."

— Thomas Edison

CHAPTER · EIGHT

Making the Switch

The most important thing to remember when changing your dog's or cat's diet is to serve the new meal with love and confidence. Instinctual reluctance to try new foods is normal. In the wild, Momdog or cat teaches her young which foods are safe and which are not. Straying from approved foods can be fatal to wild youngsters. Many domestic dogs and cats retain this instinct to varying degrees. If you put down a bowl of food that you are not confident about, your pet may be reluctant to try it. Your dog or cat can read subtle changes in your body language better than you can. You must convey to your pet that its new food is safe and healthy, and that you fully approve of it. Have patience. Many pets will switch to their new diet without any reluctance; others will take more patience and perseverance.

Some people have switched their pets to a homemade diet without any real transition. One day the dog or cat ate commercial food products, and the next they changed to homemade without any problems. You may try this approach, or you may want to ease your pet into the new diet by gradually switching foods.

To do this, make a very small complete meal of the new food, and add a tiny bit of it to the old diet. Over the course of a week to ten days, gradually add more of the homemade meal and less of the old diet until your pet is eating just the homemade diet. During this transition, smash the raw chicken or turkey necks with a hammer or mallet before feeding; then as the week progresses, smash or chop them less.

If you have an animal with a digestive or bacterial problem, or one that is or has been on antibiotics, you should add a digestive enzyme made for dogs and cats, and a non-dairy probiotic to the food for a few weeks to help replenish enzymes and friendly intestinal flora. Actually, these two healthy supplements may be used with any animal to aid the transition. They are especially useful if your pet experiences loose stools and/or gas.

Organic, raw, unfiltered apple cider can also help digestion and is especially helpful for pets that need aid with calcium utilization. Give one tablespoon per 50 pounds of pet.

Feeding a combination of homemade food and commercial food is not recommended for any longer than it takes to make the transition, about a week to ten days, possibly longer for some pets. Cats may need a little of a favorite old food mixed in with the new food for longer than dogs. If you have a particularly stubborn animal, you may want to look into using flower essences to help their transition; ask at a local health food store. Be sure to pick up the food dish after meal-time, and do not leave food out all day. To avoid digestive upsets, do not feed whole meaty bones and commercial food at the same time. Crush the bones until your pet is eating only raw food. If your pet takes longer than average to switch diets, have patience, confidence, and relay a good attitude—at least you're headed in the right direction!

Once your dog or cat is eating a nutritious, species-appropriate diet, you may notice a few changes. Some pets begin their new diet with great enthusiasm and appetite. In fact, you may become worried that you can't keep up with this new increased appetite! Have patience. Your pet may be making up for nutritional deficiencies—once they're fulfilled, consumption will decrease.

In fact, eventually you may notice that your pet needs to eat less raw food than she or he did on a commercial diet, because the raw food is so nutrient-dense that less is needed by the body. You may also notice a change in body shape, because raw food will build good muscle. You may see muscles you never knew your pet had!

Another good change will be in stool volume and consistency. The nutrients in raw food have a high bioavailability for your dog and cat, so you may notice less stool volume. Depending on the meal ingredients, you may also notice that stools are firmer and lighter in color. Firm stools are normal and naturally help express anal glands. An extra bonus is that they are easier to clean up and also faster to biodegrade. If your pet's stools are too hard or they seem constipated, adjust the ratio of stool-loosening and stool-firming foods. Bones and below-ground veggies are usually firming. Above-ground veggies, fat/oil, and vitamin C are loosening. If you find bits of undigested bone in the stool, add apple cider vinegar as described above.

Once they're eating their yummy homemade diets, some pets decide that they just want to eat their favorite part of the meal—the meaty bones. Like many human children, they'll see if they can manipulate you into giving them only "dessert" for dinner. If they refuse to eat their prepared meal because they're holding out for meaty bones, pick up their dish, put away the bones, and serve again at the next regular meal time. If you enforce the rule that no one gets their meaty bones unless they eat the rest of their meal first, they'll soon come around and eagerly eat their entire meal. It's important that they consume all the meal ingredients.

Just like us, some pets may develop personal preferences for particular foods. It's okay to cater to this, as long as it is appropriate food within the food groups, and you are still including a good variety. Do not feed an unbalanced diet in an effort to see your pet clean its dish. Always keep the prey-animal model in mind. Good eating habits are partly trained by reinforcement, either intentional or not. Once they're eating good food and their nutritional needs are being met, some pets prefer to eat less often than every day. As long as they maintain good health and condition, this is acceptable, and in fact, is very "natural."

Detoxification

When your dog or cat begins to eat nutritious raw food, the nutrients in the food will give its body enough strength to do some serious healing or "detoxing." Some pets never show any symptoms of detoxification. But in case yours does, you should be aware that the signs include discharges, pimples and rashes, loose and/or mucusy stools, bad breath, dirty ears, and body odor. Old problems may make a brief reoccurrence while deep healing takes place. The more "garbage" your pet has inside its body, the more intense the detoxification will be.

Detoxification is good as it allows your pet to rid itself of toxins, leaving the body much cleaner and healthier. Detoxification symptoms vary according to the individual. During detox, you may notice stools containing mucus and parasites. Hurrah—it's not in your pet's body anymore! Detox time varies with the individual and its toxin load, but a few days to a few weeks is normal.

If your pet is pregnant and you suspect that she may experience a great deal of detoxification, you may not want to overload her system at this time. It may be a good idea to wait until she has delivered her young before changing her diet.

During detoxification, there are ways to make your pet more comfortable. Rinsing your dog with cool water helps wash away discharges. Put a cup of organic raw apple cider vinegar in a bucket of cool water, and work it into the coat after thoroughly wetting the dog. Do not rinse it off; it removes toxins and soothes the skin.

Cats may not enjoy a rinse, but brushing them will help in a similar manner. If your feline friend is not accustomed to being brushed, begin slowly and do only a small area at a time. Try to make it a loving experience, not stressful. A little Rescue Remedy or Calming Flower Essence applied directly by mouth or rubbed into ear leather may help your cat remain calm during grooming. These remedies may also be combined with water in a spray bottle and lightly misted onto your pet's coat before brushing. Ask at your local health food store for these products.

Brush your dog or cat often during detoxification and thoroughly rinse the brush between sessions. Keep the ears clean with a warm washcloth dipped in a 50/50 mixture of water and organic, raw, apple cider vinegar, or use a good herbal ear wash.

Massaging your pet can also increase circulation and aid detoxification. Plus, it feels good! If your pet is new to massage, begin slowly; gradually increase the time and the area being worked. Do not hold your breath when you massage your pet! Sometimes we concentrate so intently on the bodywork that we don't realize we are not breathing normally. This can really stress our pet and defeats our effort. While massaging your dog or cat, breathe normally and talk in soothing tones.

Do not massage too firmly. Do what is comfortable and pleasing to your animal. Eventually, your goal should be to gently massage every part of your pet's body. Massage is a wonderful diagnostic tool, and it creates a nice bond with your furry friend.

"When the minds of the people are closed and wisdom is locked out, they remain tied to disease."

— Huang-Ti, 2696–2598 B.C.
(from the *Nei Ching Su Win*,
oldest medical book extant)

CHAPTER • NINE

Pregnancy, Puppies, and Kittens

The Ultimate Diet offers your pregnant pet wonderful nutritional benefits. When your mother-to-be begins to bloom, her stomach will be cramped for space, and you'll need to split her meals from one per day into two or three smaller meals per day. Raw food is so nutritious that you'll probably notice only a slight increase in her appetite—certainly not double, as is sometimes recommended for pets fed commercial food. Increase meat, bones, and veggies proportionately, but don't push her to eat more than she is comfortable with. Be sure she gets some raw beef or calf liver (the best is from drug-free, organically fed cows) mixed with her meals several times weekly. Liver is rich in nutrients, including folic acid—an important one for the new babes. It is also a good source of the fat-soluble vitamins A and D. Because cod-liver oil also contains these vitamins, you may cut back on the cod-liver oil if increasing her liver consumption. Review the mom-to-be's diet to be sure you haven't left anything out.

Do not fast pregnant pets. Make sure she eats ample raw meaty bones, and don't be surprised if she stashes a few in her nest for her forthcoming babies; that's what many moms do to make sure there will be food later. A couple days before her babies are due to be born, make Mom's meals slightly more laxative by feeding fewer stool-firming foods (bones, below-ground veggies, etc.) and more stool-loosening foods (liver, above-ground veggies, etc.). Don't leave ingredients out; simply alter the proportions a bit just before delivery time. During birth, allow Mom to consume the nutrient-rich placentas, and make sure each newborn drinks Mother's first milk, colostrum.

Stock up on raw, meaty bones for after the babies are born; nothing makes rich milk for growing youngsters faster. Mom will most likely have an increase in appetite when lactating to keep up with the nutritional needs of her rapidly growing young; adjust amounts of food accordingly. If she has a large litter, continue to feed her two or three times a day until it's time to wean the youngsters, at about four weeks. The exact time to wean really depends on the individual mom and growth rate of the young.

Don't be in a hurry to wean; rely on Mom to tell you when. Some mothers don't begin weaning until the young are six to eight weeks old. This is fine and gives the young more opportunity to gain good nutrients from Mother's milk. If the youngsters nurse this long, don't neglect to feed Mom more to keep up with milk production.

If she has ample milk, but a small litter, you may actually need to decrease her food so that she doesn't produce too much milk. When babies drink too much from a heavily lactating mom, they can get upset tummies and loose stools. They may cry after eating. A good tummy rub and a little peppermint and/or ginger tea through an eye-dropper (just a little, a few drops at a time) will help make them feel better.

Sometimes a new mother may also have a loose stool from cleaning up after the newborns. She may enjoy some peppermint and/or ginger tea and a tummy rub also. Some mothers may want to stash meaty bones in the nest after the babies are born. In this case, you may be feeding her too much or you may need to chop or smash them up to convince her to eat them when she's fed.

Some mothers prefer to eat in the nest at the very beginning. This is fine if it doesn't cause any animosity toward her young. Mothers who consume many placentas may not be hungry right away. Because she's a new mother, cater to her individual needs a bit.

As weaning progresses, you'll need to decrease her meals back to one a day. If, for some reason, you need to hand-feed pups or kittens, raw goat milk (organic is best) from a reputable dairy is the next best thing to Mom. Add a powdered probiotic. As soon as they are able, the young may be weaned onto solid food. If your nursing Mom has had to take any antibiotics, be sure to add a non-dairy probiotic to her food at least until the young are weaned.

In the wild, a mother animal shares her own food with her young during the weaning process. On her own, an adult *Canis lupus* eats a meal and then regurgitates it for the youngsters. Some domesticated dogs retain this instinct. If you can stomach it (pardon the pun), go ahead and let nature take its course. Momcats who hunt bring prey animals home for weanlings to eat, first dead, then alive. At some point, you'll need to assist with weaning.

The meal for weaning consists of all the same ingredients as a regular adult meal, just smaller, mushier, and with added digestive enzymes and non-dairy probiotics. These last two products can be obtained at a health food store, or through the list of products in the Resource Guide at the back of this book. Make a small complete meal, adding enough warm water to make it just a little softer than usual. The chicken necks will need to be put through a meat grinder, either at your butcher's or at home. There are modern electric grinders or old-fashioned hand-cranked ones. Either type works fine; the hand-cranked ones just take a bit more human muscle.

Mix the ground neck with the rest of the meal. Add a small amount of a good-quality powdered digestive enzyme and non-dairy probiotic. As weaning progresses, gradually go from using ground necks to thoroughly smashed necks to whole necks. Serve meals slightly warm or at room temperature. Put Mom out of the way, so she isn't a distraction, and don't attempt to feed youngsters right after they've nursed. Wait until they're hungry.

Don't forget how tiny young pup and kitten stomachs are; be careful not to overfeed. They should not look like they're about to explode after eating! During weaning, pups may be fed a small homemade meal three to four times per day; feed kittens four to six meals per day. After they're done eating, let Mom back in with them to clean them up and finish any leftovers. Don't let food dry on their coats.

A big raw-beef knuckle bone can be left in the nest for gnawing practice and fun (even cats enjoy it) as long as Mom doesn't get possessive and nasty about it. If she does, you'll need to remove it when she is there and replace it when she leaves. Cut off any really big hunks of fat from the bone before giving it to very young pups or kittens.

By the time the young are ready to go to their new homes, they should be eating whole necks and regular meals with all the extras, and you may discontinue the enzymes and probiotics (although they may help counteract the digestive stress a youngster endures when going to a new home). Youngsters may be fed three times per day from eight weeks until four to six months old, then twice daily from four to six months old until one year of age, and once daily after one year of age.

Giant breeds of dogs may need to be fed twice daily occasionally during growth spurts from one to three years of age. Either feed two complete meals or one complete and one of meaty bones (bones with ample meat) only. Observe your pet and adjust amounts accordingly.

Do not feed so much that the stomach becomes overly extended. Do not let your pet become obese. A very thin layer of fat over the ribs is healthy, but too much weight puts extra stress on growing bones, joints, and hearts. A healthy wild animal is a lean animal. If your pet needs to lose weight, reduce its food intake. If it needs to gain weight, increase its food. Keep in mind that growing youngsters will eat more per pound of body weight than adult animals.

All animals need daily exercise for proper health, but do not force youngsters to overexert themselves. In the wild, youngsters run, jump, and play a lot, but in short bursts and at their own speed on natural surfaces. Do not allow young animals to jump down from high places or to race about on slick tiled floors.

On the other hand, you won't do your youngster any favors by restraining it from normal daily exercise. Exercise is needed to build healthy muscles and sound bodies. Good muscle tone is especially important to joint health. If your pet spends a lot of time indoors, you will need to enforce safe daily exercise in the fresh air outside. Use common sense and supervision. Daily exposure to sunshine is also important, but be certain to always supply access to shade and water.

"If we eat wrongly,
No doctor can cure us;
If we eat rightly,
No doctor is needed."

— Victor G. Rocine

CHAPTER TEN

Senior Citizens

As wild dogs and cats grow older, their diets do not change. They continue to thrive by eating prey animals and a few extras. The wild diet provides them with a wide variety of easily absorbable nutrients. The veterinary community has debunked the theory that good protein contributes to kidney dysfunction. It is the quality of protein that is crucial. Feed your older pet optimal amounts of high-quality protein, such as raw meat, fish, and eggs, balanced within the homemade diet. The Ultimate Diet provides good nutrition for domesticated pets of any age. Most older pets retain much more energy and youthfulness on a species-appropriate diet of homemade food. But when your pet does begin to slow down, you'll need to adjust the amount of food accordingly so that they do not gain extra unhealthy weight. Do not let your pet become obese. Obesity is very hard on your pet's bones, joints, and heart. As long as your pet is mobile, it will benefit from daily exercise and fresh air. This is especially important to remember in multiple-pet homes because sometimes a younger pet may monopolize your time and energy.

If you have an older pet that you wish to switch to the Ultimate Diet, you may need to make a few adjustments depending on the condition of your mature friend. If your senior citizen has very few teeth, you may need to feed raw bones in ground form. There are home grinders, or you may have your butcher grind them for you. Depending on the condition and past health history of your older pet, it may experience a lot of detoxification when changed to good food. Read the information on detoxification to learn how to help your pet remain comfortable during this healing transition. Also, you may want to switch your older pet to its new diet slowly and with the help of non-dairy probiotics and digestive enzymes. A bit of fresh ginger mixed with the veggies can aid protein digestion and acts as a natural anti-inflammatory. Organic, raw, unfiltered apple cider vinegar is a good addition to the meal for pets with calcification of joints. If you have a senior citizen with serious health problems, you may wish to consult an experienced veterinary practitioner for assistance. Many older pets have turned back the clock when switched to the Ultimate Diet. It's never too late for good health!

"Nobody can be in good health if he does not have fresh air, sunshine, and good water."

— Flying Hawk, Oglala Sioux Chief

CHAPTER ELEVEN

General Guidelines

- Prepare and serve your pet's meals with love and confidence.

- Provide safe exercise daily.

- Provide safe exposure to daily sunlight and fresh air.

- Feed healthy, non-pregnant, non-lactating adult animals one meal daily.

- Do not leave food out between meals (exception: occasional raw knuckle bone).

- Serve food at room temperature.

- Rotate—use a variety of suggested foods within each food group.

- Use only stainless steel or lead-free glass and ceramic dishes for food and water.

- Do not microwave your pet's food or store it in aluminum foil.

- Good-quality drinking water should be available at all times.

- Pulp vegetables thoroughly.

- Do not feed heated, rancid, or hydrogenated oils and fats.

- Fast healthy, non-pregnant, non-lactating adult animals once weekly.

- Never feed cooked bones.

- Do not leave any suggested ingredients out of the diet.

- Store oils in the refrigerator, and shake very gently before using.

- Handle meat as you would for yourself; clean surfaces, refrigerate, etc., but do not poison your pet with cleaning chemicals.

- Do not encourage hard exercise after eating.

- Avoid unhealthy treats.

- Give extras in powdered form whenever possible.

- Do not allow your pet to become overweight.

- Use a natural dust-free litter in cat boxes, not a "clumping" one.

- Seek help from a qualified veterinary practitioner when needed.

"This we know.
The earth does not belong to man;
man belongs to the earth.
This we know.
All things are connected
like the blood which unites one family.
All things are connected.
Whatever befalls the earth
befalls the sons of the earth.
Man did not weave the web of life;
he is merely a strand in it.
Whatever he does to the web,
he does to himself."

— Chief Seattle

CHAPTER•TWELVE

Species-Appropriate Sources of Nutrients

 All nutrients are important to health. They interact with each other and work together to keep your pet happy and healthy. Nutrients don't work alone; they work in harmony with each other within the body. Raw food is a great source of natural nutrients with superior bioavailability. The following table lists nutrients vital to your pet's health, along with the species-appropriate foods to find them in, and which parts of the body that particular nutrient supports. The following list is not all-inclusive. Foods listed are raw; organically grown, non-irradiated food is preferred.

NUTRIENT	SPECIES-APPROPRIATE FOOD SOURCE	BODY PARTS, SYSTEMS, AND ORGANS
Vitamin A	alfalfa, cod-liver oil, eggs, fruit, fish, kelp, meat, meaty bones, vegetables	*bones, hair, immune and respiratory systems, skin, soft tissue, teeth*
Antioxidants	bilberry, cod-liver oil, fish, fruit, nuts, vegetables, vitamin C	*cells, free-radical damage, heart, immune system, joints*
Vitamin B complex	alfalfa, eggs, fish, fruit, kelp, meat, meaty bones, veggies, nuts, seeds	*cells, eyes, gastrointestinal tract, hair, liver, nervous system, mouth, skin*

NUTRIENT	SPECIES-APPROPRIATE FOOD SOURCE	BODY PARTS, SYSTEMS, AND ORGANS
Bioflavonoids (vitamin P)	algae, fruit, berries, rose hips	*blood, capillary walls, connective tissue, red blood cells, teeth*
Biotin	alfalfa, eggs, fish, fruit, kelp, meat, nuts	*bone marrow, genes, glandular and metabolic systems, hair, muscles, skin*
Boron	fruit, nuts, vegetables	*bones, brain, muscles*
Vitamin C	alfalfa, fruit, kelp, meat, meaty bones, vegetables	*adrenal glands, blood, bones,capillary walls, cells, connective tissue, heart, mucous membranes, nervous system, teeth*
Calcium	alfalfa, bones, carob, eggshell, kelp, vegetables	*blood, bone, heart, muscles, nails, skin, soft tissues, teeth; circulatory, digestive, enzymatic, immune, and nervous system*
Carbohydrates	fruit, vegetables	*brain, energy, nervous system*
Choline	eggs, fish, kelp, meat, nuts, seeds, vegetables	*adrenal glands, brain, kidneys, liver; cardio-vascular, glandular, and nervous systems*
Chromium	alfalfa, vegetables, fruit, kelp, meat, meaty bones, nuts, seeds	*adrenal glands, brain, blood, heart, liver, white blood cells, circula-tory and immune systems*
Copper	alfalfa, avocado, fish, kelp, nuts, meat, meaty bones, seeds, vegetables	*blood, bone, circulatory system, hair, skin*
Vitamin D	alfalfa, cod-liver oil, eggs, fish, meat, meaty bones, sunlight	*bones, eyes, heart, kidney, glandular and nervous systems, skin, teeth*

NUTRIENT	SPECIES-APPROPRIATE FOOD SOURCE	BODY PARTS, SYSTEMS, AND ORGANS
Vitamin E	alfalfa, eggs, fish, kelp, meat, meaty bones, nuts, seeds, vegetables	*arteries, circulatory, heart, nervous and glandular systems, heart, lungs, skin*
Enzymes	raw foods	*all biochemical activities*
Vitamin F	alfalfa, kelp, nuts, seeds, vegetable oils	*cells, glands, hair, mucous membranes, nerves, skin*
Fat	animal skin and fat, avocados, eggs, fish, meat, nuts, oils, poultry, seeds	*brain, energy, insulation, liver, blood, nervous system, nutrient utilization*
Fluorine	garlic, kelp, vegetables	*bones, blood, lymphatic system, teeth*
Folic acid	alfalfa, eggs, fish, fruits, meat, vegetables	*blood, glands, liver, reproductive system*
Inositol	fruit, kelp, meat, nuts, seeds, vegetables	*brain, hair, heart, intestines, kidneys, nerves, skin*
Iodine	alfalfa, eggs, kelp, fish, meat, meaty bones	*brain, glandular system*
Iron	alfalfa, eggs, fish, kelp, meat, meaty bones, vegetables	*blood, bone, metabolic system, muscles, nails, skin, teeth*
Vitamin K	alfalfa, cod-liver oil, eggs, fish, kelp, vegetables	*blood, bone, liver, gastrointestinal system*
Love	human and animal friends	*all biochemical activities*
Magnesium	alfalfa, fish, fruit, kelp, meaty bones, seeds, vegetables	*arteries, bones, cells, heart, nerves, teeth; digestive, immune, nervous, and reproductive systems*

NUTRIENT	SPECIES-APPROPRIATE FOOD SOURCE	BODY PARTS, SYSTEMS, AND ORGANS
Manganese	alfalfa, berries, eggs, kelp, meat, meaty bones, nuts, seeds, vegetables	*blood, bones, brain, immune system, liver, mammary glands, muscles, nerves*
Molybdenum	alfalfa, kelp, vegetables	*bones, cells, kidneys, liver, nitrogen metabolism*
Phosphorus	alfalfa, eggs, fish, kelp, meat, meaty bones	*bones, brain, eyes, liver, muscles, nerves, teeth; circulatory and digestive systems*
Potassium	alfalfa, dates, fish, fruit, kelp, meat, meaty bones, vegetables	*blood, heart, kidneys, muscles, skin; endocrine, digestive, and nervous systems*
Protein	eggs, fish, meat, nuts, poultry, seeds	*acid/alkaline balance, energy, fluid balance, hair, hormones, immune system, muscles*
Selenium	alfalfa, eggs, fish, garlic, kelp, meat, meaty bones, vegetables	*enzyme and immune systems, eyes, heart, pancreas, red blood cells, tissue elasticity*
Silicon	alfalfa, kelp, meaty bones, vegetables	*arteries, bones, connective tissue, hair, heart, nails, skin*
Sodium	alfalfa, eggs, fish, kelp, meat, meaty bones, vegetables	*blood, lymphatic system, muscles, nerves*
Sulfur	eggs, fish, garlic, kelp, meat, meaty bones, vegetables	*blood, cells, liver, skin, soft tissues*

NUTRIENT	SPECIES-APPROPRIATE FOOD SOURCE	BODY PARTS, SYSTEMS, AND ORGANS
Sunlight	direct sunlight (not through windows)	*vitamin D absorption*
Vitamin T	eggs, sesame seeds	*blood, immune system*
Vitamin U	cabbage	*intestines, skin, tissues*
Vanadium	fish, kelp, meat, meaty bones	*bones, cellular metabolism, heart, kidney, teeth*
Water	distilled or reverse osmosis (other sources should be tested for quality)	*nutrient absorption, circulation, digestion, excretion*
Zinc	alfalfa, eggs, fish, kelp, meat, meaty bones, nuts, seeds	*blood, bones, eyes, heart, joints, liver*

"Let food be thy medicine."

— Hippocrates

CHAPTER·THIRTEEN

Your Tribe

Β y changing your pet's diet in the ways discussed, you can join the ever-growing "tribe" of those who have already traveled a path similar to the one you're on now. You are not alone; there are thousands of dog and cat guardians all over the world who successfully feed their animals a homemade diet of raw species-appropriate foods. So, my friends, listen now to their stories. Gather 'round the fire in the company of your fellow tribespeople as they tell you of their beloved pets; let's begin with Epic, a beautiful Newfoundland.

Epic

We called him the nuclear Newf. A mischievous puppy, an irascible adolescent, Epic, whose full title is Seaworthy's Epic Tide, CD, WRD, DD, eventually matured into a powerful working dog; he tackled obedience, carting, and water rescue with raging enthusiasm. But after he turned five, still prime time for a Newfoundland, our amazing powerhouse began to slow down. His chin turned gray, his coat dulled, and he seemed to be losing that unique *joie de vivre* that was his alone. I was alarmed. It was too soon for Epic to be getting old. After all, my friend Kymythy had two female Newfs only a few months younger, and they still looked and acted like pups: glowing coats, clean teeth, full of energy and fun.

I suspected the difference had something to do with nutrition. Kymythy fed her girls an all-natural, homemade diet based on raw meat. It was a concept that intrigued me, but I had no idea what to feed a Newf, I worried about salmonella and E. coli, and I was a disaster in the kitchen. Consequently, Epic had always dined on the very best commercial dog food available.

But I'd always wondered: *Was it really enough?* My nuclear Newf was a lean, mean, working machine, weighing in at around 140 pounds. How could his every nutritional need possibly be fulfilled by a daily bowl of cereal? Plus, he'd always been a picky eater, and even though I switched brands occasionally to pique his interest, eventually they all bored him. I grew to dread that crestfallen look that followed his every hopeful peek into the dog dish. And now he was aging before my eyes.

It was time to talk turkey (literally) with Kymythy. I asked a lot of questions. She had a lot of answers. In the end, it all made sense. So I made a decision: Epic was going to eat real food. My family couldn't believe it. "You don't even cook for us," they said, "and you're going to make dog food every night?"

"I'm just going to try it," I countered. Still they scoffed. But it didn't take long for the big experiment to pay off. Within two weeks, Epic was wriggling with energy again. He seemed spunkier, healthier, happier. It was obvious he just plain felt good. After three weeks, even the family skeptics had noticed the difference. Epic was back!

Things just got better from there. This year, his seventh, Epic has seemed younger in every way than he did at five. His teeth are clean and white. His coat is thick and shiny. His personality sparkles, and he's always ready for action. Carting, swimming, hiking, tracking, agility, obedience, or just a quick walk around the block: Epic still does it all with style and enthusiasm. What's more, my formerly picky eater now relishes his supper. Apparently, real food isn't just good for you; real food tastes good, too!

— Sandra Younger

Julius and Vito

I have two wonderful kitties; Julius is five, and Vito is two. They have both been raised on a raw food diet. When I got Vito as a very young kitten, he wasn't in very good health. He had a bloated stomach and smelled very bad. It was apparent that he had not received proper nutrition. He was pulling his hair out under his neck and on his rear. I immediately started giving him Rescue Remedy and fed him the Ultimate Diet. It wasn't hard to convince him to eat the new diet when he discovered that after he finished his meat, veggies, and extras, he got dessert—chicken necks. Raw chicken necks are the best thing in the world to Julius and Vito. They love them so much, in fact, that they devised a plan to get them whenever they felt like it! Vito would act as the lookout, while Julius opened the refrigerator door and pulled out the necks. Then the feast began! We've had to make some special alterations to the refrigerator, and now the necks are safely kept out of reach until dessert time.

Julius and Vito are indoor cats with sleek and shiny coats. I can't tell you how many visitors are amazed at their obvious good health. Many of them admit that my cats smell a lot better than their own! I'm very proud of my natural furbabies. I have healthy, happy kitties, and I owe it all to the Ultimate Diet and lots and lots of love.

— Sarah Maio

∽ ∽

Skeeter and Belle

My dog Skeeter had always had a dry, harsh coat. I tried giving her coat conditioners, but nothing ever helped. When she came into her first heat, she lost patches of hair all over her body. The vet diagnosed it as generalized mange and advised me to have her spayed, because he said that, even if she healed, she would suffer a reoccurrence with each heat cycle. He also said that some dogs never recover from an advanced case such as Skeeter's, and many have to be euthanized. My heart was broken. I began the recommended course of ointments and dips. After two dips, I decided to change her diet to a homemade one of raw foods. In less than three weeks on her new diet, she was healed! Her coat is now wonderfully healthy, and she has had no reoccurrence of the mange, even while in heat. My other dog, Belle, has also benefitted from the diet. Belle's vet had advised me to have her teeth cleaned, but after only two weeks on the species-appropriate diet, her teeth looked so great that the vet thought they had already been cleaned elsewhere! Also, after two months on the diet, Belle's previously low thyroid tested normal.

Being a nurse, I have seen first-hand the good and the bad of modern medicine. Being an experienced dog person, I know that one must also think for oneself. I could not be more convinced that a species-appropriate diet of raw foods is the right thing to feed my dogs. Thank you, Kymythy, for all the time and knowledge you have shared.

— Betty Amezola

Topper

I started researching diets when one of my dogs, Topper, developed calcium oxylate stones and had to have surgery to remove them. He was 14 months old and I had never before had that problem, in almost 30 years of working with dogs. When the vet wanted to put him on a commercial food that I dislike, I started looking for an alternative. I began feeding a better quality commercial diet, but felt the dogs were still missing something. When a friend mentioned that she fed naturally, I started questioning her. I had already read a few books on the subject, so I decided to take the plunge. The dogs now eat all raw food with no grains, dairy, or yeast. They are happy, healthy dogs with beautiful coats, and Topper's last blood work was perfect. I think this diet saved his life and allowed him to continue showing. Hopefully, he will soon produce his first litter. It's a good thing I switched to his current diet—this boy is so vain, he would have died without the beautiful hair it has enabled him to grow!

— Charlotte Merrifield

ᴥ ᴥ

Tabasco, Barbeque, Roy Biggins, and Diamond

Because I want the best for my animals, I chose to switch them from a kibble diet [that is, a diet of commercial dog food] to a species-appropriate one. It was easy going at first; throw a chicken wing on top of the kibble and I was done. However, I got more and more into feeding naturally, so I started adding more things and reducing the kibble, until I decided one day that since I was adding a complete meal to kibble each day—why bother with the kibble?!

I stopped, and immediately my cats and dogs looked and acted so much better. I had the support of my friends on the Internet, who helped me tweak the diet to be as pure as I can get it. Kymythy helped in so many ways, especially by pinpointing the cause of my dog's hacking. She went through the ingredients one by one and offered suggestions; several weeks later I realized that I hadn't heard one hack from my dog. This was after seeing several veterinary specialists, by the way.

The natural diet has also prevented my cat Roy from blocking again. His urinary tract had been blocked twice, which can be fatal, before I put him on a species-appropriate diet. I believe that this diet saved his life. I am now trying to get others in my area interested in feeding naturally and giving their pets a better life, which is important to me, as I hope to be a veterinarian someday.

— Tiffani Beckman

❧ ❧

Chamonix, Cousteau, Ysabeaux, and Navarre

Like most new dog owners, we fed our Newfoundland Chamonix "dog food." On that commercial food, however, she suffered through itchy and scabby skin, diarrhea, and urinary tract infections; also, she was bothered constantly by fleas, which led to tapeworms. All these problems, of course, led to lots of trips to the vet and lots of bills! Chamonix was a very picky eater, too. It would take her hours to finish her meal, and we'd wait and watch her because we worried about bloat.

Everything has changed since we began feeding Kymythy's recommended diet. Chamonix now has a beautiful shiny coat, no scabs, no itches, and *no fleas*. She loves what she's eating now, and eats her meal as soon as it hits her bowl; we no longer wait, watch, and worry about bloat.

Our cat Navarre suffered very much the same problems as Chamonix. However, our cat Ysabeaux was healthy and flea-free. We wondered how that could be since she often slept next to Navarre. Well, she was eating her own species-appropriate diet! She ate very little at home, instead preferring to hunt and eat mice and birds. When we switched the cats to the new diet, Navarre's problems cleared up and Ysabeaux started eating all her meals at home.

Our latest addition, Cousteau, is another Newfie, and has been on Kymythy's diet from the day we got him. He has not had any medical problems. Cousteau is an extremely healthy, bright, happy puppy who loves his food.

For us and our very special furry loved ones, this diet has made all the difference in their well-being. We tell everyone we know how wonderful it is. You must try it!

— Chance and Jeanine Geurin

❧ ❧

Sarah, Ben, Pudge, Bear, and Minnow

From the day I got Sarah, my cocker spaniel, she had health problems. She suffered from ear infections, stomach upsets, and diarrhea. By the time she was a year old, she also had flaking, oozing sores all over her underside. The vet's treatment consisted of antibiotics and steroids, which cleared it up only temporarily. Her last outbreak covered her entire body, and the vet wanted to put her on permanent medication. I opted to change her diet instead. Since she has been eating a species-appropriate diet of raw foods, all her health problems have cleared up with no reoccurrence.

My other dogs have enjoyed similar benefits on their new diet. My bichon, Ben, also used to suffer from ear infections and diarrhea. His problems have now disappeared. Bear, my Newf/malamute cross, was a real mess. He was skinny and lethargic; he coughed and had runny eyes and nose. Today he is a totally new dog! He is fit and energetic, with clear eyes, good skin, and shiny white teeth (all the dogs' teeth now look great). My dog Pudge was born with a congenital defect in his rear legs, but don't tell him! On his new diet he has endless energy, a strong front, bright eyes, and an amazingly shiny coat. I believe this diet is keeping him strong and healthy enough to compensate for his congenital problems. My latest rescue dog is Minnow, a Newf with cardiomyopathy. In one week's time on her new diet, she has gained needed muscle tone, and her frequent water consumption and urination have normalized. Because of her heart problems, Minnow may not live long, but I firmly believe that this diet will give her an optimal quality of life for the time she has left.

— Jane Richter

Taylor

In January 1997, I acquired my eight-year-old champion male Yorkshire terrier, Champion Durrer's Whims 'n' Wishes (Taylor), for what amounted to less than a stud fee. I soon found out why; he had chronic colitis and emotional problems. I tried many different commercial "specialty" foods for him, and nothing worked to stop the chronic diarrhea and obvious discomfort he felt a lot of the time. When I was told by a previous owner that it had been common for her to come into the dog's room in the morning and find a big pool of bloody diarrhea, it really scared me. There had to be something I could do for him!

Unfortunately, my vet was of no help at the time, so I read everything I could get my hands on. I found the book, *Dr. Pitcairn's Complete Guide to Natural Health for Dogs and Cats,* as well as the Wellpet mailing list. Taylor began to improve in leaps and bounds, but still something was amiss. Then I joined the Newleaf and Critterchat mailing lists. During one of the "chats" that Kymythy was hosting, I questioned her about Taylor's problems, and she kindly and carefully explained that dropping grains and dairy was probably the way to go.

I thought it over for a couple days (it's hard to break years of conditioning) and then had the choice taken away from me one day by the dog himself. He absolutely refused his usual breakfast, and at supper time I was frantic to get him to eat. I warmed up the meat and veggie mix, without grains, and fed it to him. He ate it all. After that, all the dogs were switched to a diet excluding grains and dairy, and are healthier because of it. But the biggest and most important change has been in my Taylor. He has gained some much-needed weight, and his coat has filled in beautifully; even the bald patches are growing hair, and he has started to emotionally interact with the family much more. He no longer snaps at everyone, and actually gives kisses and cuddles to the kids!

I took pictures of Taylor to show to one of his previous owners, and she was stunned; she had last seen him when I picked him up in January. She picked up the picture and said, "Now, who is this?" I told her that it was Taylor, and she couldn't believe it, saying, "You've done wonders with him!" I told her that his colitis and diarrhea had also cleared up. It was great to realize that someone else could also see the change in him, and to know that I had helped.

— Jean Clement

Halle

Halle, our German shepherd/hound cross, was ten years old when we switched her to a species-appropriate diet of raw foods. Before we switched, her teeth had been completely encased in a rock-hard green coating that the vets wanted to remove. I couldn't bring myself to put her under anesthesia to do it. Within three days of starting the raw diet with bones, there were a few tiny white spots on her teeth. Now, after six months, her teeth are shiny white with almost no discoloration on them at all. Another positive change has been in her behavior. She has gone from spending most of her time lying behind the dining room table with no interest in anything, to playing with the pup and being her rascally self. She used to avoid all human contact and had to be begged and pleaded with to eat her kibble. Now, she comes around frequently for pats and *inhales* her raw food. And that's in addition to her shiny coat and bright eyes. Even her lipomas are disappearing! She is a dramatic example of the good that this diet can do.

— Barb Johnson

Harley and Ashley

In August 1991, I brought home my first naturally fed puppy. The pup was beautiful—bright and healthy. My husband was nervous about feeding him raw meat and chicken bones, especially since he was only eight weeks old. After about a week, my husband demanded that I feed the pup a dry commercial food, so I reluctantly switched him to a top brand. After about two weeks on the kibble, the hair on our pup's rear end started falling out, and he had developed a bad odor. During this time, I had been learning more about commercial and homemade diets. I insisted that we stop feeding him kibble and place him back on his breeder's raw diet. We switched him back, and he immediately began to improve. Switching him back to raw food was the best thing I ever did for him. Today, he is a very happy, healthy dog. He is now seven years old, and I am proud to say that the only time he has ever needed to visit a veterinarian was to be neutered.

I now have a second-generation raw-food dog. She is one of the most intelligent dogs I have ever known. I can't help but compare my two dogs to kibble-eating dogs; but really, there is just no comparison. My dogs have shiny thick coats and bright white teeth (with no brushing). They smell fresh and healthy. And we simply don't have vet bills. I believe that my dogs deserve the best care that I can give them, and that includes a raw food diet. It really is the Ultimate Diet! I love knowing exactly what they're eating. It is a joy to watch them chow down their food and listen to them crunch their meaty bones, because I know it brings them good health. I want to thank Kymythy for teaching me how to have healthy dogs.

— Jackie Helland

❧ ❧

Shelby, Auberon, Paedyn, Eliot, and Aislinn

My soulmate is a rottie named Auberon. From the beginning, he had terrible reactions to vaccines and commercial food. As I began to educate myself about holistic veterinary medicine, I decided to make my animals' meals at home; eventually, I put all my pets on a diet of raw foods. Auberon's health has improved immensely, and he has put on some much-needed weight. The other dogs and my cats love their new diet, and all the animals have more energy. My 12- and 15-year-old cats are like kittens again.

In a way, Auberon's health problems were a blessing in disguise, because they forced me to think for myself, stop being coerced by advertising, and find a better way for my pets. I thank my little Aubie-man for that!

— Leslie Wiens

❧ ❧

Tiger, Snuggles, and Wrigley

After much consideration, I decided to switch my three cats to Kymythy's recommended homemade diet. Before that time, my orange cat Tiger was very skittish and afraid of everything. He also regularly threw up his commercial food at least once a week. My girl cat, Snuggles, had previously had most of her teeth removed because they had rotted, plus she had terrible breath. The family called my other cat "psycho cat" instead of by his name, Wrigley, because he was so vicious. He had once been hospitalized with urinary crystals and was eating a very expensive cat food that the vet had recommended. His coat was awful: dull, thin, and extremely oily.

It took the cats about a month to totally accept their new homemade diet; now they *love* it. I have the butcher grind Snuggle's chicken necks since she has few teeth to mash them with. The boys eat theirs without any problem. The change in their health has been astounding. Tiger is no longer afraid of everything and no longer vomits his food. Snuggle's bad breath is completely gone, and Wrigley is now "the wonder cat" instead of "psycho cat." He cuddles, loves everyone, and rides around the house on my shoulders. He has not had any health problems since he's been eating his homemade food. All of the cats' coats are full, rich, and luxurious. Switching my cats to the Ultimate Diet is the best thing I've ever done for them.

— Natalie Lynn Clark

The Springhaven Newfoundlands

This past year I made the decision to change my dogs' diet back to one that included a commercial kibble. For about 14 years before that, I had been feeding a raw foods/natural diet without kibble or processed foods. During that time, my dogs and those I bred achieved great success in the show ring. In addition to championship and obedience titles, I also produced multiple best-in-shows, group winners and placers, specialty winners, and the number-one Newf in the U.S. for two years.

When I decided to change their diet, I used kibble as a base and continued to add a variety of fresh foods daily, keeping the amount of additions to no more than 15–20% of the diet. At first, it seemed to be going well, although a few of the girls were getting a bit chubby. But then I started to notice that some of the kids were getting "gunky ear syndrome." In the past, on a totally natural diet, I had never had any ear infections or problems. Ears were always sweet-smelling and clean. On the kibble, several of the dogs progressed to full-blown infections, scratching hair off near their ears. They also had a few hot spots, which I hadn't experienced in many years. One of the girls even chewed herself until she had sores on her front legs. I also noticed hair missing around the dogs' eyes and a loss of black pigment on their noses. The most painful part of the kibble experiment was the dog that bloated and died. In 22 years, I had never had a dog bloat. It was my first experience, and I keep wondering if I may have contributed to it by adding kibble to their diet.

Needless to say, I have thrown away the kibble, and have gone back to natural feeding. I have proven to myself that there is no substitute for natural food and the health that it brings. What I find most interesting about this experience is that I knew my dogs did better when I switched them to a natural diet, but seeing it from this perspective really reinforced the difference it makes in their health. I think people who say that their dogs are just as healthy on a kibble-based diet have simply come to expect the assortment of ills that come along with it as being part of dog ownership, and don't have a clue that it is diet-related.

— Joanne Givens

Lara

Lara had chronic ear problems and sebaceous cysts before we changed her diet. I got her when she was three and a half years old and discovered that her breeder had been giving her low doses of prednisone for a long time. When the drug was discontinued, she developed allergy problems, ear infections, and discharges, as well as lots of scratching. All tests were negative; the vets diagnosed her as "just having allergies."

I changed her food to a popular "natural" diet, and her cysts disappeared after a few months; however, she developed the most awful hot spots. And her ears were still a problem. Then I decided to drop all grains and dairy from her diet. Two months later, her ears were clean! I couldn't remember the last time her ears looked so good. Poor dog, I kept grabbing her and peering into her ears, because I just couldn't believe it! Too bad it took me so long to get it right. Lara is now 12 years old—at least she finally has healthy ears!

— Regina Steiner

Digby and Heidi

My Tibetan terrier, Digby, was quite successful in agility competitions as a young dog. But at age eight, he was getting arthritic and was not keen on jumping. About two years ago, I changed his diet to a more natural one, but he was still very stiff in the mornings. The big change came when I dropped the grains and dairy from his meals; he began to bounce around like a puppy again! He now has no soreness and even won a small recent agility competition.

Heidi is another eight-year-old Tibetan terrier. For several years, she had persistent sebaceous cysts. Now, on her species-appropriate diet of raw foods, all the cysts have vanished, and she has a really fantastic coat. Like her brother, Digby, she also has a renewed vigor in her agility work. My thanks to Kymythy for recommending that we give up grains and dairy; it's given my dogs a new lease on life.

— Jane Heritage

❧ ❧

Muffin and Chloe

"If only" . . . how many times have we said that? For years I battled with a chronic skin complaint that made my German shepherd/greyhound's life a misery. Only when I switched her diet from commercial to homemade did her problems begin to improve. But months later, she was still not completely healed, and the open sores on both her paws remained stubbornly angry. Muffin had seemed to reach a certain level of improvement, but obviously we still had some way to go in our search for a complete cure. I began to study nutrition for dogs in earnest. Then I spoke with Kymythy, and she gave me her diet recommendations. I decided to try it for a month, just to see if it would make any difference. The rest, as they say, is history. I was astounded by the obvious healing process happening before my very eyes. Muffin's skin became supple, pink, and healthy; a soft, silky, thick coat soon followed. Her legs, so long an eyesore in every sense, quickly became perfect again. At 15 years of age, she was finally healed.

Cats need raw bones, too. Chloe is a very stubborn Russian blue. Before I switched her to a species-appropriate diet, she had begun losing weight, her coat was sparse, and she had generally lost interest in life. I looked forward to her improved health on a diet of raw foods, including raw chicken necks—but Chloe had other ideas. At first, she hated her new diet! It took the competition of a new puppy to convince her to try the new food. Once she'd had a taste, she was convinced, and now she eagerly consumes a diet of raw meaty bones, pulped veggies, kelp and alfalfa, and some oils. She feels great and looks like the cat I always wanted.

— Anna Carr-Twinberrow

Sacre-Tyana Salukis

Salukis are supposed to be long-lived, and I often congratulated myself on choosing a breed so healthy. I could attribute any problems to fate and get on with my life. Then the problems began to multiply until, finally, I had a bitch with a wound that would not heal, and I began to wonder if I had been living in a fool's paradise.

A change to "better" dog foods "healed" this bitch, but my days of oblivion were past. The next seven years consisted of studying dog food bags; with each change, I would see temporary improvement of their overall condition, but the dogs never reached what I could consider "good" health. Finally, I began cooking grains for them and adding raw meat and vegetables.

It was as though I had stood with my dogs outside a garden of indescribable beauty. Sometimes we could see into the garden, but we were never allowed inside—until we stumbled onto a species-appropriate diet. Suddenly, problems that I'd always considered "normal," such as runny ears and occasionally thin coats, became a problem for other people's dogs, not mine. I'm now showing and winning with dogs of an age most people would retire. Their coats are vibrant with health and have a depth of color seldom seen— I can't wait for our next litter.

Then there's the cat. After 15 years of "correct" commercial foods, he faced old age with a dysfunctional liver and a diet restricted to food he refused to eat. The only solution seemed to be "letting him go," since I couldn't bear to watch him starve. We switched to a species-appropriate diet; now he spends his nights purring in my ear.

Veterinarians tend to disparage a diet not formulated at a large sterile factory, and I'm sure many other owners are convinced I've gone insane . . . let 'em mock.

— Monica Henderson Stoner

❧ ❧

Orangewood Rhodesian Ridgebacks

My husband and I live with eight wonderful Rhodesian ridgeback dogs. We show the dogs in conformation, they lure course, and we breed an occasional litter. You could say that the dogs are the center of our lives.

In the past, I fed a "natural" kibble diet with veggies and cooked (sometimes raw) meat. The dogs all seemed healthy and all looked good. Yet, I was always looking for something better to feed. I strive to give my dogs the best-quality life I can provide, and the idea of feeding a raw diet interested me greatly. I just didn't know how to get started, and frankly, the idea of feeding raw bones (as natural as they are) was a little intimidating.

I had looked at a few books on the subject, but I still hesitated until I attended one of Kymythy's workshops on species-appropriate nutrition. That was my turning point; it made all the sense in the world to me. We started following her recommendations right away, and I'll never go back to any other way of feeding. Our guys love every morsel and lick their bowls clean. It is amazing to watch them "crunch crunch," using their neck and jaw muscles the way they were meant to.

The dogs' coats look great, teeth are cleaner than before, and muscle tone and vitality have increased. Before the new diet, our five-year-old male named Junior had decided that the couch was all the activity he needed, kinda old before his time. You should see him now! He is "young" again and having a ball.

We are planning a litter of pups in the spring, and they will be fed a species-appropriate diet upon weaning. I am very excited at the prospect of rearing pups on food they are meant to eat.

— Deborah Adams

❧ ❧

Taiga, Keisha, Tikki, Taffeta, and Zeikiah

My Tibetan terriers have experienced many positive changes in health, including sparkling white teeth, lots of energy, and better coats since switching to a species-appropriate diet of raw foods. My seven-year-old, Taiga, had really slowed down before the diet change. He had previously been on prednisone after a surgery and always had no fewer than four or five cysts on his body. Now, he has a new zest for life, and his cysts are almost completely gone. Then there's Taffeta, who had always had very irregular heat cycles. On the new diet, she is cycling normally, and we hope to breed her soon. Another dog, Tikki, has stopped chewing her back feet, and her hair is growing in again. Most exciting is the improvement in Tikki's nose pigment, which has changed from an undesirable light to a wonderful dark color. My husband, joking, teased that I had colored her nose with crayon!

It only takes me about 10 to 15 minutes a day to prepare the species-appropriate diet, serve it, and clean up after five dogs. I feel that this is a very small amount of time to give for all the advantages that both they and I receive.

— Linda McCue

❧ ❧

Violet and Maggie

In the past, I was never one to think about what my dog ate—unless it was a pair of my favorite shoes! I just did what all the dog food companies told me to do, which was to feed my dog a pile of dry stuff. It was very convenient. I did notice, however, that for every cup of dog food eaten, it seemed that my dog was able to double the volume that I had to pick up in the yard.

All that changed when my family learned that the breeder we were getting a new puppy from required that the pup be fed a homemade diet. In order to prepare for the pup's arrival, we started our older dog on the new diet. After learning about this different way to feed my dogs, I admit that I was overcome with guilt about the way I had been feeding. The new way made much more sense to me. Let's face it—if your dogs were in charge of feeding *you,* and all they ever did was give you a bowl of dried hard stuff to eat, you probably wouldn't be very happy either.

Now, after two years of feeding my dogs the Ultimate Diet, they are healthier and happier than ever. They have beautiful shiny coats and are full of energy. When I put their food bowls down, they are eager to eat and don't give me that "Oh, not this stuff again" look. The homemade diet does take a little more time and effort to prepare than just pouring kibble in a bowl, but the long-term health benefits and the happiness of the dogs make it worthwhile. My dogs depend on me for their health and well-being, and I feel so good knowing that I do the best I can for them.

— Bob Lyon

"There is life on earth—one life,
which embraces every animal and plant on the planet.
Time has divided it up into several million parts,
but each is an integral part of the whole.
A rose is a rose, but it is also a robin and a rabbit.
We are all of one flesh, drawn from the same crucible."

— Lyall Watson

✠ *Conclusion* ✠

Sometimes, a frustrating aspect of feeding a homemade diet are the incredulous looks, imploring questions, and thoughtless accusations you may receive from people to whom it is a foreign concept. Some people have never considered the notion that a pet would enjoy fresh, wholesome food just as they do. Many people consider all whole foods to be "people food," even though animals actually ate it before humans evolved into "humans"! The media is a strong force in our society these days, and advertising has helped to convince many people that commercial products are the only acceptable option for feeding pets.

Even many veterinarians have had little to no unbiased nutritional education. In 1997, *The Wall Street Journal* reported that, outside universities, a particular multi-million dollar pet food company was the largest employer of veterinarians, which makes nutritional impartiality rather difficult. Fortunately, there are some doctors who have made the extra effort to learn more about animal nutrition for themselves and their clients. And there are even some who will welcome your assistance in helping them to learn more.

To keep the concept of feeding a homemade diet in context, you may want to remind people that dog and cat lovers all over the world have been keeping their pets in good health with homemade meals for thousands of years. After all, what did people do before commercial products were invented? Many people from older generations will understand completely. It is the way they raised animals when they were young. You're simply caring for your furry friends the "old-fashioned" way! The commercial foods are actually the "new" stuff. Homemade diets are the "traditional" way to feed dogs and cats. If you look in some of the older breed books, you'll find well-respected dog and cat authorities recommending raw homemade diets for pets. Many generations of good veterinarians also recommended it. It simply used to be the "normal" way to feed dogs and cats. In fact, many old-timers have never changed their methods and continue to feed a homemade diet because it works so well for them. No one seems to question the use of homemade diets for humans; in fact, most doctors highly recommend them for better health! By preparing a homemade diet for your dog or cat companion, you're simply making a healthy meal for another member of your family.

You'll find comrades through the Internet, newsletters, books, workshops, lectures, schools, and many other sources. And the number is growing all the time. As more people become dissatisfied with their pet's poor health, more of them are seeking nutritional information to help build a foundation for good health. And as more caring pet people seek nutritional information to help improve their own lives, the more they will learn how to apply that knowledge to improve the well-being of their animal companions.

Holistic Health

The term *holistic* has become very trendy these days. But the concept is really quite simple. Holistic care embraces your pet as an organic being with a reality greater than just the sum of its individual parts. No one single part of your pet's body is more important than another, because all the parts depend on each other to survive. Every part is connected to every other part. Your pet's heart or hips are not more important to its body than the eyes or lungs. The glandular system does not work independently from the circulatory system. All parts and all systems are connected and work together to keep your beloved pet healthy and happy. The holistic view also incorporates genetic predisposition, mental, emotional, and environmental factors that affect your pet. It looks at the big picture—what affects the whole animal. Nutrition is the foundation of holistic health care, because it supplies nourishment or "fuel" for the entire body. Poor-quality food supplies poor fuel. Good-quality food helps the body perform to the best of its ability. If you have any doubt that food affects well-being, you could try not eating any food for a month and see if you feel affected—but I don't recommend it!

As important as good nutrition is, please do not discount the other factors that affect your pet's health. Drugs, poor water, x-rays, and toxins (even the ones that are used so commonly that you don't think about it) can seriously affect your pet's health. Even your own illness and emotions affect your animal friends.

The information in this book is really as old as our furry friends themselves. Sometimes it just takes a bit of mind-tweaking and species detective work for us humans to go beyond our own hang-ups, and see what is really appropriate for our animal friends. They are not human and should not be fed as such. *But, they are also not less deserving than us, and should not be fed as such.*

If holistic care for pets is new to you, I'd like to encourage you to read some of the many good books available on the subject, some of which are listed in the back of this book. You'll find that there are many marvelous modalities that are safe and effective to encourage optimum health in your cat or dog. They complement a solid foundation of good nutrition. It's easy to feel overwhelmed by all the information, so you may want to choose one area at a time to study in depth. Seek other like-minded animal lovers to exchange information with and to boost your confidence. And don't forget to listen to your own common sense and to your heart. Remember, no one knows your cat or dog better than you do. There are many fantastic resources for you available through books, videos, and practitioners. I greatly appreciate all the authors, veterinarians, consultants, and animal lovers for their effort to help people help their pets. Anything we learn that brings us closer to our animal friends and enables them to live an optimal quality of life contributes to the well-being of us all.

✒ *Appendix* ✒

Shopping List ✣

Muscle and organ meat—for example: ground/minced poultry, beef, or lamb muscle meat; organ meat such as liver, gizzards, etc.; eggs

Bones—for example: chicken necks or backs; turkey necks

Vegetables—for example: carrots, sweet potatoes, broccoli, squash, celery, parsley, ginger, garlic, wheatgrass

Essential fatty acids—for example: cod-liver oil; as well as fish body oil, flaxseed oil, or hemp seed oil

Kelp and alfalfa—in finely powdered form

Vitamin C—for example: calcium or sodium ascorbate

Snacks and treats—for example: large beef knuckle bone; raw, unsalted nuts and seeds (pecans, almonds, pumpkin, sunflower); fruit

Optional—organic apple cider vinegar; digestive enzymes; non-dairy probiotics; citrus seed extract

Approximate Amounts ⚘

The amounts listed below are offered to give you a general idea only, and should be used as a *loose* guide, with one exception: Do not use more than the recommended amount of cod-liver oil. It contains the fat-soluble vitamins A and D, and although both are of vital importance to health, they are stored by the body and may be toxic if overdosed.

Just like humans, the amount of food needed by an individual can vary widely. The amount of food your pet needs depends greatly on the individual animal, including its metabolism, age, breed, exercise level, temperament, environment, and such factors. Meat and bone amounts vary depending on type and size of meaty bones fed. For example, raw turkey or chicken wings and legs provide more muscle meat than necks. If the bones contain a lot of meat, you may need to decrease other muscle meat fed. Even the same item from different locales can vary in size.

Include a small amount of organ meat several times weekly, unless you are feeding chicken backs, which usually come with organ meat attached. Also include eggs a few times per week. Vegetables can be increased or decreased depending on bowel tolerance and pH. Bones firm an animal's stools, and veggies loosen them. If your pet consumes a lot of animal fat, oils may be decreased. You know your pet better than anyone else. Watch stools and overall physical and mental condition to determine diet adjustments.

If your pet leaves food, give less at the next meal. If your pet devours the food and begs for more, increase the portion.

Also adjust amounts to obtain your pet's ideal weight. Keep an eye and a hand on your pet to determine if amounts need to be increased or decreased. Always keep the wild diet and the prey-animal model in mind to help you correctly balance food groups. Amounts listed are per day.

The vitamin C levels listed are based on the work of Wendell O. Belfield, D.V.M. (see the Resource Guide for his books). In times of stress, you may want to use vitamin C to bowel tolerance. To do this, begin with a low dose and gradually increase the amount of vitamin C until it creates a loose stool. Return to the previous dose that did not create a loose stool. That is how much your dog or cat needs at that time. The dosage may be increased in times of stress and illness, and decreased for maintenance. Always reduce dose gradually.

Pet's weight: **10 lbs.**

1. **Raw meat:** $1/4$–$1/2$ cup muscle meat
   (plus organ meat or egg)
2. **Raw bone:** 1–2 chicken necks
3. **Veggies:** $1/2$–1 tbl, pulped
4. **Kelp/alfalfa:** $1/2$–1 tsp
   Cod-liver oil: $1/4$ tsp
   EFAs: $1/2$ tsp
   Vitamin C: up to 500–1,500 mg

Pet's weight: 50 lbs.

1. **Raw meat:** 3/4–1 cup muscle meat
   (plus organ meat or egg)
2. **Raw bone:** 1 turkey neck or 6 chicken necks
3. **Veggies:** 3 tbl, pulped
4. **Kelp/alfalfa:** 2 tsp
   Cod-liver oil: 1 tsp
   EFAs: 2 tsp
   Vitamin C: up to 3,000–6,000 mg

Pet's weight: 100 lbs.

1. **Raw meat:** 1 1/2–2 cups muscle meat (plus organ
   meat or egg)
2. **Raw bone:** 2–3 turkey necks
3. **Veggies:** 1/4–1/2 cup, pulped
4. **Kelp/alfalfa:** 1 tbl
   Cod-liver oil: 2 tsp
   EFAs: 1 1/2 tbl
   Vitamin C: up to 6,000–7,500 mg

Sample Monthly Menu

Sunday	Monday	Tuesday	Wednesday	Thursday	Friday	Saturday
Your food choices may vary due to local availability, preference, compatibility, condition, and size of dog or cat. Always keep the prey animal model in mind and use a variety of ingredients within that ideal. Monitor your pet's condition and adjust diet accordingly. This menu is a loose guide only.				**1** beef & egg turkey necks carrot/yam/ celery/parsley/ garlic/extras	**2** beef & liver turkey necks carrot/yam/ celery/parsley/ garlic/extras	**3** beef & liver turkey necks carrot/yam/ celery/parsley/ garlic/extras
4 fast day good drinking water only	**5** turkey & egg turkey necks potato/carrot/ dandelion/squash/ ginger/extras	**6** turkey & liver turkey necks potato/carrot/ dandelion/squash/ ginger/extras	**7** turkey & liver turkey necks potato/carrot/ dandelion/squash/ ginger/extras	**8** turkey & liver turkey necks potato/carrot/ dandelion/squash/ ginger/extras	**9** turkey & egg turkey necks potato/carrot/ dandelion/squash/ ginger/extras	**10** a whole chicken
11 fast day good drinking water only	**12** turkey & egg chicken backs swt potato/beet romaine/thyme/ garlic/extras	**13** turkey chicken backs swt potato/beet romaine/thyme/ garlic/extras	**14** turkey & egg chicken backs swt potato/beet romaine/thyme/ garlic/extras	**15** a whole chicken	**16** turkey & egg chicken backs swt potato/beet romaine/thyme/ garlic/extras	**17** turkey chicken backs swt potato/beet romaine/thyme/ garlic/extras
18 fast day good drinking water only	**19** whole fish	**20** beef & liver turkey necks carrot/yam/ mint/broccoli/ ginger/extras	**21** beef & liver turkey necks carrot/yam/ mint/broccoli/ ginger/extras	**22** beef & egg turkey necks carrot/yam/ mint/broccoli/ ginger/extras	**23** beef & egg turkey necks carrot/yam/ mint/broccoli/ ginger/extras	**24** beef & liver turkey necks carrot/yam/ mint/broccoli/ ginger/extras
25 fast day good drinking water only	**26** turkey & gizzards chicken necks potato/carrot/ celery/romaine/ ginger/extras	**27** turkey & gizzards chicken necks potato/carrot/ celery/romaine/ ginger/extras	**28** turkey & egg chicken necks potato/carrot/ celery/romaine/ ginger/extras	**29** turkey & gizzards chicken necks potato/carrot/ celery/romaine/ garlic/extras	**30** whole rabbit	

Menu ✑

Anything new requires time and repetition to become a habit. The sheets that follow will help your new diet plan more quickly become an easy habit. Make a few copies of the following menu sheet, fill one out, and post it where you can see it in the feeding area. At first, you'll need to look at it often to remember all the ingredients. Eventually, you'll know it by heart, and preparation time will be minimal.

Pet's name: _____

Feed _____ times per day at_____o'clock.

Raw meat:_____
Raw bone:_____
Raw veggies:_____
Kelp/alfalfa: _____
EFAs:_____
Vitamin C:_____
_____
_____

Assemble all ingredients. Pulp vegetables. Combine ingredients in bowl with warm water to bring to room temperature. Make food mushy, not soupy. Give raw bones for dessert or with meal. Do not encourage hard exercise after eating. Feed non-pregnant, non-lactating adults over one year of age one meal per day. Feed weaned youngsters two to three times per day. Fast non-pregnant, non-lactating, healthy adult animals over one year of age one day per week. Fast youngsters six months and older a half day once per week. Provide clean, good-quality drinking water at all times. Serve food and water in lead-free ceramic, glass, or stainless steel dishes.

Additional instructions:

_____
_____
_____
_____
_____
_____
_____

Food Diary ☙

Pet's name: _____ Age:_____

Before Diet Change:
(examine your pet closely and describe condition of the following areas)

Nose:_____

Teeth and gums:_____

Eyes: _____

Ears: _____

Skin:_____

Coat: _____

Muscle tone: _____

Stools: _____

Behavior:_____

_____

_____

Exercise routine: _____

_____

Notes and observations: _____

_____

_____

_____

_____

Current diet:_____

Your goals for this pet: _____

_____

_____

_____

Date of Transition to the Ultimate Diet: _____

Date diet change is complete: _____

Date and symptoms of detoxification, if any:_____

_____

_____

_____

Favorite foods: _____

Least favorite foods:_____

Health Improvements—include date_____
(examine your pet closely and describe condition of the following areas)

Nose:_____

Teeth and gums:_____

Eyes:_____

Ears: _____

Skin: _____

Coat: _____

Muscle tone:_____

Stools:_____

Behavior: _____

_____

_____

Exercise routine:_____

_____

Notes and observations:_____

_____

_____

   Periodically review the diet to make sure you're not leaving anything out and that your balance is correct. Make copies of the Menu Sheet and update as needed. Date and save old copies for reference. Remember, deep healing can take time; be patient and observant. Always seek professional medical advice if needed.

The Holistic Animal Resource Guide ✐

These resources are for your personal information and enjoyment. No endorsements of any kind are implied. Readers are urged to thoroughly research qualifications, compatibility, and quality of health care providers and products for their furry friends.

Associations & Organizations

Academy of Veterinary Homeopathy
1283 Lincoln Street
Eugene, OR 97401
(541) 342-7665

The American Botanical Council
P.O. Box 201660
Austin, TX 78720
(512) 331-8868

American Holistic Veterinary Medical Association
2214 Old Emmorton Rd.
Bel Air, MD 21015
(410) 569-0795

American Veterinary Chiropractic Association
623 Main St.
Hillsdale, IL 61257
(309) 658-2920

Animal Protection Institute of America
P.O. Box 22505
Sacramento, CA 95822
(800) 348-7387

Association of Holistic Animal Practitioners
P.O. Box 500335
San Diego, CA 92150
(619) 223-0658

British Homoeopathic Association
27A Devonshire St.
London W1N 1RJ England
071-935-2163

The British Institute of Veterinary Homeopathy
520 Washington Blvd., #423
Marina Del Rey, CA 90292
(800) 498-6323

Florida Holistic Veterinary Medical Association
751 Northeast 168th St.
North Miami Beach, FL 33162-2427
(305) 652-5372

**Greater Washington Area
Holistic Veterinary Association**
6136 Brandon Ave.
Springfield, VA 22150
(703) 503-8690

The Herb Research Foundation
1007 Pearl St., #200
Boulder, CO 80302
(303) 449-2265

**International Association for
Veterinary Homeopathy**
334 Knollwood Ln.
Woodstock, GA 30188
(770) 516-5954

**International Veterinary
Acupuncture Society**
268 West Third St., Suite 4
Nederland, CO 80466-2074
(303) 449-7936

Natural Pet Products Association
P.O. Box 355
Conner, MT 59827
(406) 821-1939

**Price-Pottenger
Nutrition Foundation**
P.O. Box 2614
La Mesa, CA 92041
(619) 574-7763

**Rocky Mountain Holistic
Veterinary Medical Association**
311 S. Pennsylvania St.
Denver, CO 80209
(303) 733-2728

Touch For Health Association
6955 Fernhill Dr., #2
Malibu, CA 90265
(310) 457-TFHA

**Veterinary Institute for
Therapeutic Alternatives**
15 Sunset Terr.
Sherman, CT 06784
(860) 354-2287

**Wisconsin Institute of Chinese
Herbology Veterinary Program**
(414) 884-9549

Books

AAFCO Publications
Georgia Department
of Agriculture
Room 604, Capitol Square
Atlanta, GA 30334
(404) 656-3637

*Acupuncture Points and Meridians
in the Dog*
by Luc Janssens

Animal Nutrition
by John D. Rowe

*Animals As Teachers
& Healers*
by Susan Chemak McElroy

Animals . . . Our Return to Wholeness
by Penelope Smith

Animal Talk: Interspecies
Telepathic Communication
by Penelope Smith

Animal Wisdom:
Communications With Animals
by Anita Curtis

Aqua Vitae: Catalyst Altered Water
by Roy M. Jacobsen

Are You Poisoning Your Pet?
by Nina Anderson &
Howard Peiper

Back to Basics
by Wendy Volhard

Bioenergetic Medicine:
Homeopathy and Acupuncture
for Animals
by Joanne Stefanatos, D.V.M.

Bone Appetit Cookbook
by Anson

Canine Acupressure
by Nancy A. Zidonis &
Marie K. Soderberg

Canine Nutrition: Choosing the
Best Food for Your Breed
by William D. Cusick

Cat Care, Naturally
by Celeste Yarnall

Cat Lover's Cookbook
by Lawson

Cat Lover's Cookbook
by Papai

Cat Massage
by Ballner

Cats: Homeopathic Remedies
by George Macleod, M.R.C.V.S.,
D.V.S.M.

Cats Naturally: Natural Rearing
for Healthier Cats
by Juliette de Bairacli Levy

Cat Treats
by Kim Campbell Thornton &
Jane Calloway

Communicating with Animals: The
Spiritual Connection Between
People & Animals
by Arthur Myers

The Complete Herbal Handbook
for Dog and Cat
by Juliette de Bairacli Levy

Complimentary and Alternative
Veterinary Medicine
by Allen Schoen, D.V.M., &
Susan Wynn, D.V.M.

Consumer's Guide to Cat Food:
What's in Cat Food, Why It's
There, and How to Choose the
Best Food for Your Cat
by Liz Palika

Consumer's Guide to Dog Food:
What's in Dog Food, Why It's
There, and How to Choose the
Best Food for Your Dog
by Liz Palika

Conversations with Animals
by Lydia Hiby

Doggie Delicacies
by Link

Dogs: Homeopathic Remedies
by George Macleod, M.R.C.V.S.,
D.V.S.M.

Dr. Jane's 30 Days to a Healthier,
Happier Cat
by Jane R. Bicks, D.V.M.

Dr. Pitcairn's Complete Guide to
Natural Health for Dogs and Cats
by Richard H. Pitcairn, D.V.M.,
Ph.D., & Susan Hubble Pitcairn

Earl Mindell's Nutrition and
Health for Dogs: Natural
Remedies and Preventive Care to
Keep Dogs Healthy and Vibrant
Throughout Their Lives
by Earl Mindell &
Elizabeth Renaghan

The Encyclopedia of Natural
Pet Care
by C.J. Puotinen

Fat Cat, Finicky Cat: A Pet
Owner's Guide to Cat Food and
Feline Nutrition
by Karen Leigh Davis

Feeding Strategy
(Survival in the Wild)
by Jennifer Owen

Feed the Kitty—Naturally
by Joan Harper

Flea Control: A Holistic and
Humorous Approach
by Sammons

Food Pets Die For
by Ann Martin

Four Paws, Five Directions
by Cheryl Schwartz, D.V.M.

Give Your Dog a Bone
by Ian Billinghurst, V.V.Sc(Hons),
B.Sc.Agr., Dip.Ed.

Grow Your Pups with Bones
by Ian Billinghurst, V.V.Sc(Hons),
B.Sc.Agr., Dip.Ed.

The Healing Touch
by Dr. Michael Fox, M.R.C.V.S.

The Health and Beauty Book
for Pets
by Linda Clark

The Healthy Cat and Dog Cook Book
by Joan Harper

Healthy Diet, Healthy Dog: How to Prevent Illness and Maximize a Dog's Health and Energy Through Nutrition
by Shawn Messonnier

Heal Your Cat the Natural Way
by Richard Allport, B.Vet.Med., et.M.F.Hom., M.R.C.V.S.

Heal Your Dog the Natural Way
by Richard Allport, B.Vet.Med., et.M.F.Hom., M.R.C.V.S.

Herbal Remedies for Dogs & Cats: A Pocket Guide to Selection and Use
by Mary Wulff-Tilford & Gregory L. Tilford

The Herb Book
by John Lust

A Holistic Approach to Cancer Treatment and Nutrition
by Joanne Stefanatos, D.V.M.

The Holistic Guide for a Healthy Dog
by Wendy Volhard & Kerry Brown, D.V.M.

The Holistic Veterinary Handbook
by William G. Winter, D.V.M.

The Homeopathic Treatment of Small Animals: Principles and Practice
by Christopher Day

Homeopathy in Veterinary Practice
by K. J. Biddis

How to Have a Healthier Dog
by Wendell O. Belfield, D.V.M., & Martin Zucker

How to Talk to Your Cat
by Jean Craighead George

How to Talk to Your Dog
by Jean Craighead George

Investigative Report on Pet Food
by the Animal Protection Institute of America

It's for the Animals! Cookbook
by Helen L. McKinnon

Keep Your Pet Healthy the Natural Way
by Pat Lazarus

Kinship with All Life
by Allen J. Boone

Let's Cook for Our Cat
by Edmund R. Dorosz

Let's Cook for Our Dog
by Edmund R. Dorosz

A Little Recipe Book for Dogs: Sound Nutrition and Good Homecooking for Your Pet
by Jaroslav Weigle

*Love, Miracles and
Animal Healing*
by Allen Schoen, D.V.M.

Natural Care of Pets
by Donald I. Ogden, D.V.M.

Natural Cats
by Madsen

The Natural Dog
by Mary L. Brennan

*Natural Dog Care: A Complete
Guide to Holistic Health Care
for Dogs*
by Celeste Yarnall

*Natural Food Recipes for
Healthy Dogs*
by Carol Boyle

Natural Healing for Cats
by Susanne Bonisch

*Natural Healing for Dogs
and Cats*
by Diane Stein

*Natural Health Care for Your
Dog: Quick Self-Help Using
Homeopathy and Bach Flowers*
by Petra Stein

Natural Immunity
by Pat McKay

Natural Insect Repellants
by Janette Grainger &
Connie Moore

*Natural Nutrition for Dogs
and Cats: The Ultimate Diet*
by Kymythy R. Schultze,
C.C.N., A.H.I.

*The Natural Remedy Book for
Dogs and Cats*
by Diane Stein

Natural Supplements for Dogs
by Shawn Messonnier

*Natural Therapy for an
Arthritic Dog*
by Shawn Messonnier

*Natural Therapy for an
Itchy Dog*
by Shawn Messonnier

The New Natural Cat
by Anitra Frazier

*No Barking at the Table
Cookbook: More Recipes Your
Dog Will Beg For*
by Wendy Nan Rees

*No Catnapping in the Kitchen:
Kitty Cat Cuisine*
by Wendy Nan Rees

Nutrient Requirements of Dogs
by National Research Council,
Subcommittee on Dog Nutrition

*Nutritional Therapy for
Dog Diseases*
by Shawn Messonnier

*The Original Gourmet Doggie
Treat Cook Book*
by Carole Laybourn

*Pet Allergies: Remedies
for an Epidemic*
by Alfred J. Plechner, D.V.M.
& Martin Zucker

Pottenger's Cats
by Francis M. Pottenger Jr., M.D.

Reigning Cats & Dogs
by Pat McKay

The Revolution in Cat Nutrition
by Jane R. Bicks, D.V.M.

*The Scientific Validation of
Herbal Medicine*
by Daniel B. Mowrey, Ph.D.

Super Nutrition for Animals!
by Nina Anderson
& Howard Peiper

Talking with Nature
by Michael J. Roads

The Tellington TTouch
by Linda Tellington-Jones with
Sybil Taylor

*Top Dog Homeopathic Emergency
Handbook for Dogs*
by Volhard & Chase

*Traditional Chinese
Veterinary Medicine*
by Xie. Huiesheng

*The Traditional Flower Remedies
of Dr. Edward Bach*
by Leslie J. Kaslof

*The Treatment of Cats by
Homeopathy*
by K. Sheppard

*Vaccination: What You Must Know
Before You Vaccinate Your Dog*
by Shawn Messonnier

Vegetarian Cats & Dogs
by James A. Peden

The Very Healthy Cat Book
by Wendell O. Belfield, D.V.M.,
& Martin Zucker

Veterinary Acupuncture
by Alan Klide & Kung Shiu

*Veterinary Acupuncture: Ancient
Art to Modern Medicine*
by Allen Schoen, D.V.M.

Veterinary Aromatherapy
by Nelly Grosjean

A Veterinary Materia Medica &
Clinical Repertory
by George Macleod, M.R.C.V.S.,
D.V.S.M.

The Well Adjusted Cat
by Daniel Kamen, D.C.

The Well Adjusted Dog
by Daniel Kamen, D.C.

What the Animals Tell Me:
Developing Your Innate Telepathic
Skills to Understand and
Communicate with Animals
by Sonya Fitzpatrick with Patricia
Burkhart Smith

Who Killed the Darling
Buds of May
by Catherine O'Driscoll

The Wolf Within: A New Approach
to Caring for Your Dog
by David Alderton

Your Cat Naturally
by G. McHattie

Your Natural Dog
by Angela Patmore

Periodicals

Canine Health Naturally Newsletter
P.O. Box 69
Lions Bay, B.C.
V0N 2E0 Canada
(604) 921-7784

Dynamis: The Journal for the
International Association for
Veterinary Homeopathy
42 rue Francis Poulenc
F-77 430 Champagne Sur Seine
France

Enchanted Connections Review
18 Josephine Ln.
Fort Salonga, NY 11768
(516) 269-7641

Healthy Pets—Naturally
1895 New Franklin Church Rd.
Canon, GA 30520
(706) 356-7031

The Holistic Dog & Cat Newsletter
P.O. Box 1717
Kingston, WA 98346
(360) 394-8338

Holistic Hound
P.O. Box 2249
Oak Park, IL 60303
(888) 219-2509

*Journal of the American Holistic
Veterinary Medical Association*
2214 Old Emmorton Rd.
Bel Air, MD 21014
(410) 569-0795

*Love of Animals: Natural Care
and Healing for Your Pets*
7811 Montrose Rd.
Potomac, MD 20854
(301) 424-3700

*Natural Rearing Breeder's
Directory Natural Rearing
Newsletter*
P.O. Box 1436
Jacksonville, OR 97530
(541) 899-2080

PetSage News
4313 Wheeler Ave.
Alexandria, VA 22303
(800) 738-4584

*Price-Pottenger Nutrition
Foundation Health Journal*
2667 Camino del Rio South,
Suite 109
San Diego, CA 92108-3767
(800) FOODS-4-U

Wellness for Pets
P.O. Box 190
Hansville, WA 98340
(360) 638-2840

The Whole Dog Journal
P.O. Box 420235
Palm Coast, FL 32142
(800) 829-9165

*Wysong Companion Animal
Health Letter*
1880 North Eastman
Midland, MI 48640-8896
(517) 631-0009

Practitioners

Practitioners listed here are not veterinarians. A list of veterinarians in
your area may be available by send-
ing a self-addressed, stamped enve-
lope to the veterinary association or
organization of desired modality.

Adams, Connie
(805) 956-6405
2308 White Ave.
Santa Barbara, CA 93109
*Animal communicator, Reiki master,
& nutritional consultant*

Alcott, Miranda
(877) 778-1817
P.O. Box 2660
Corrales, NM 87048
*Animal communicator &
certified TTouch practitioner*

Bell, Kristen
(877) 894-2283
180 St. Paul St., #402
Rochester, NY 14604
Certified aromatherapist

Brinks, Gesa
(909) 928-0836
Equine body work

Debono, Mary
(619) 223-0658
P.O. Box 500335
San Diego, CA 92150
Certified animal massage therapist
& Feldenkrais practitioner

Dewar, Laurie
(403) 431-0559
#5 10025 84th Ave.
Edmonton, Alberta T6E 2G6
Canada
Animal bodywork & holistic care
consultant

Guerrero, Diana
(800) 818-7387
P.O. Box 1154
Escondido, CA 92033
Animal behaviorist

Hiby, Lydia
(909) 926-4748
33240 Leon Rd.
Winchester, CA 92596
Animal communicator

Jordan, Robert
(508) 385-4549
P.O. Box 795
East Dennis, MA 02641
Animal homeopath

Kansoer, Patrick C., Sr.
(773) 274-2447
P.O. Box 555
Winnetka, IL 60093-0555
Holistic companion
feline consultant

Khury, Samantha
(310) 374-6812
1251 10th St.
Manhattan Beach, CA 90266
Animal communicator

Lewis, Betty, RVT, Dr. A.N.
(603) 673-3263
17 Danbury Circle
Amherst, NH 03031
Animal communicator & holistic
animal consultant

Lingrey, Terry
(707) 445-5721
1221 H Street
Eureka, CA 95501
Holistic animal care consultant

McKay, Pat
(818) 296-1122
396 West Washington Blvd.
Pasadena, CA 91103
Animal nutritionist

Meyers, Barbara
(718) 720-5548
29 Lyman Ave.
Staten Island, NY 10305
Certified grief therapist & Bach
flower counselor

Miller, Debbi Parshall, N.D.
(440) 474-4505
5939 Trumbull Road
Geneva, OH 44041
Naturopathic doctor & animal
care consultant

Morris, Francine
(512) 338-4509
9600 Glenlake Drive
Austin, TX 78730
Certified TTouch practitioner

Noel, Brigitte
(619) 295-5504
P.O. Box 33857
San Diego, CA 92163-3857
Animal communicator

Saleh, Kim
(613) 836-3881
1250 Main Street
Stittsville, Ont.
K2S 1S9 Canada
Homeopathic consultant

Schultze, Kymythy, C.C.N, A.H.I.
(360) 394-8338
P.O. Box 1717
Kingston, WA 98346
Certified clinical nutritionist &
animal health instructor

Worden, Caryl
(250) 743-1913
1771 West Shawnigan Lake Rd.
Shawnigan Lake, B.C.
V0R 2W0 Canada
Researcher & desktop publisher

Yarnall, Celeste, Ph.D.
(310) 278-1385
Animal nutritional consultant

Products

A Drop in the Bucket
586 Round Hill Rd.
Greenwich, CT 06831
(888) 783-0313

All the Best Pet Care
8050 Lake City Way
Seattle, WA 98115
(800) 962-8266

Alternatives for Animals
Referral Service
P.O. Box 1641
Brighton, MI 48116
(800) 424-8044

Ambrican: Complementary
Health Care Products
for Breeders
P.O. Box 1436
Jacksonville, OR 97530
(541) 899-2080

**Anaflora: Flower Essence
Therapy for Animals**
P.O. Box 1056
Mt. Shasta, CA 96067
(916) 926-6424

Animal Food Services, Inc.
675 E. State Street
Iola, WI 54945
(800) 743-0322

Animal Natural Health Center
1283 Lincoln St.
Eugene, OR 97401
(503) 342-7665

Animal's Apawthecary
P.O. Box 212
Conner, MT 59827
(406) 821-4090

Aromaleigh, Inc.
180 St. Paul Street #402
Rochester, NY 14604
(877) 894-2283

Avena Botanicals
20 Mill St.
Rockland, ME 04841
(207) 594-0694

Ayush Herbs, Inc.
(800) 925-1371

**Barbara's Canine Catering
& Dog Cafe**
(888) K9-TREAT

Best Friends MSC #B-6
7621 Firestone Blvd.
Downey, CA 90241-0470
(310) 928-6799

Blessed Herbs
109 Barre Plains Rd.
Oakham, MA 01068
(508) 882-3839

Boericke & Tafel
2381 Circadian Way
Santa Rosa, CA 95407
(800) 876-9505

Boiron Borneman
6 Campus Blvd., Ste. A
Newtown Square, PA 19073
(800) BLU-TUBE

Bow Wow Meow
1415 North 45th St.
Seattle, WA 98103
(206) 545-0740

Brunzi's Best
RR1 Box 63
Garrison, NY 10524
(914) 734-4490

**Cut-Heal Animal Care
Products, Inc.**
923 South Cedar Hill Rd.
Cedar Hill, TX 75104
(800) CUT-HEAL

Deep Sea Harvesters, Inc.
P.O. Box 1561
Lewiston, NY 14092
(888) 4-DEEPSEA

Designing Health
28410 Witherspoon Pkwy.
Valencia, CA 91355

Dexter's Deli
1229 Camino Del Mar
Del Mar, CA 92014
(619) 792-3707

Dog & Cat Book Catalog:
Direct Book Service
P.O. Box 2778 / 701B Poplar
Wenatchee, WA 98807-2778
(800) 776-2665

Dolisos America, Inc.
3014 Rigel Ave.
Las Vegas, NV 89102
(702) 871-7153

Dr. Goodpet
P.O. Box 4489
Inglewood, CA 90309
(800) 222-9932

Earth Animal
606 Post Road East
Westport, CT 06880
(800) 622-0260

Earthrise Animal Health
P.O. Box 459NP
Tollhouse, CA 93667
(800) 995-0681

Earth Seasons Herb Company
P.O. Box 461198
Escondido, CA 92046
(760) 740-1746

EHP Products, Inc.
P.O. Box 1306
Ashland, KY 41105-1306
(606) 329-9339

Ellon Bach, USA, Inc.
644 Merrick Rd.
Lynbrook, NY 11563
(800) 433-7523

Equine Acupressure, Inc.
(888) 841-7211

Essentially Yours Industries
12115 Dermott
Houston, TX 77065
(888) 719-0901 or
(281) 894-0046

Fleabusters Rx for Fleas
10801 National Blvd.
Los Angeles, CA 90064
(800) 846-3532

Flora, Inc.
P.O. Box 950 / East Badger Rd.
Lynden, WA 98264
(800) 498-3610

Flower Essence Services
P.O. Box 1769
Nevada City, CA 95959
(800) 548-0075

4M Dog Books
1280 Pacific St.
Union City, CA 94587
(800) 487-9867

Frontier Cooperative Herbs
P.O. Box 299
Norway, IA 52318
(800) 786-1388

Gentle Wind Designs
(510) 283-3190

Halo
3438 East Lake Rd., #14
Palm Harbor, FL 34685
(800) 426-4256

Happy Pet
709 Taraval St.
San Francisco, CA 94116
(415) 566-2952

Harmony Veterinary Products
3065 Center Green Drive, #140
Boulder, CO 80301
(800) 481-4433

Healing Herbs for Pets
4292-99 Fourth Ave.
Ottawa, Ontario K1S 5B3
Canada
(888) 775-PETS

Herbal Alternatives
3507 Tully Rd., #E2-55
Modesto, CA 95356-1052

Herb Pharm
P.O. Box 116
Williams, OR 97544
(800) 348-4372

Homeopathic Educational Services
2124 Kittredge St.
Berkeley, CA 94704
(800) 359-9051

**Homeopathic Resources
and Services**
P.O. Box 131
Old Chatham, NY 12136

IG Hawaii, Inc.
94-1061 Alelo St.
Waipahu, HI 96797
(808) 677-1624

Indian Books & Periodicals
P.O. Box 2524, B-5/62, Dev Nagar
Pyare Lal Road, Karol Bagh,
New Delhi 110005 India

**Karidan's Natural
Pet Care Products**
1980 Elm Tree Terrace
Buford, GA 30518
(888) 697-9374

K.R. Natural Pet's
(800) 200-7890

Love Your Pet Products
P.O. Box 260129
Encino, CA 91426
(800) 323-3369

Mary Dahout's Natural Ways
1926 Bonus Dr.
San Diego, CA 92110
(888) 275-8893 or
(619) 275-2293

Merritt Naturals
P.O. Box 532
Rumson, NJ 07760
(888) 463-7748

The Minimum Price Homeopathics
P.O. Box 2187
Blaine, WA 98231
(800) 663-8272

The Natural Pet Care Catalog
8050 Lake City Way
Seattle, WA 98115
(800) 962-8266

Natural Remedi's
5939 Trumbull Road
Geneva, OH 44041
(440) 474-4504

Naturmix USA, Inc.
P.O. Box 682
Cumming, GA 30128
(770) 781-8190

Naturvet
27461-B Diaz Rd.
Temecula, CA 92590-3410
(888) 628-8783

Nelson Bach USA, Ltd.
100 Research Dr.
Wilmington, MA 01887
(800) 314-BACH

Noah's Ark
6166 Taylor Rd., #105
Naples, FL 34109
(941) 592-9388

Norfields Magnetics
$632^3/4$ North Doheny Dr.
Los Angeles, CA 90069
(800) 344-8400

North Star Natural Pet Products
RR 1, Box 428B-NP
Tinmouth, VT 05773
(802) 446-2812

Odyssey Formulas
RD #1 135C, Rt. 11 Unit 4
Northumberland, PA 17857
(800) 206-1861

The Ohio Hempery, Inc.
P.O. Box 18
Guysville, OH 45735
(800) 289-4367

Omega Nutrition USA, Inc.
6515 Aldrich Rd.
Bellingham, WA 98226
(800) 661-3529

Optissage
(800) 251-0007

Orthomolecular Specialties
P.O. Box 32232
San Jose, CA 95152-2232
(408) 227-9334

Pat McKay, Inc.
396 West Washington Blvd.
Pasadena, CA 91103
(800) 975-7555

Pet Botanics
710 South Ayon Ave.
Azusa, CA 91702
(818) 969-3797

Pet Friend
3441 Cortese Dr.
Los Alamitos, CA 90720
(800) 219-8361

Petsage
4313 Wheeler Ave.
Alexandria, VA 22304
(800) PET-HLTH

Pet's Friend, Inc.
7154 N. University Dr., #720
Tamarac, FL 33321
(800) 868-1009

Pet World International, Inc.
5201 Spice Drive
Palm Beach Gardens, FL 33418
(800) 780-7954

PHD Products, Inc.
P.O. Box 8313
White Plains, NY 10602
(800) 863-3403

P.O.R.G.I.E. Natural Pet Supply
2023 Chicago Ave., B-25
Riverside, CA 92507-2311
(909) 784-9070

Prozyme Products, LTD
2567 Greenleaf Ave.
Elk Grove, IL 60007
(800) 522-5537

Solid Gold Health Products
1483 North Cuyamaca
El Cajon, CA 92020
(619) 258-7356

Source, Inc.
101 Fowler Rd.
North Branford, CT 06471
(800) 232-2365

**The S'petacular Dog Snack
Company**
3820 Wilkinson Blvd.
Charlotte, NC 28208
(704) 372-7363

Springtime, Inc.
10942-J Beaver Dam Rd. /
P.O. Box 1227
Cockeysville, MD 21030
(800) 521-3212

**Standard Homeopathic
Company**
P.O. Box 61067
Los Angeles, CA 90061
(800) 624-9659

Standard Process Labs
P.O. Box 904
Palmyra, WI 53156
(800) 558-8740

Steve's Real Food for Dogs
3070 McKendrick St.
Eugene, OR 97405
(888) 526-1900

Stittsville IDA Pharmacy
1250 Main St.
Stittsville, Ontario
K2S 1S9 Canada
(613) 836-3881

Summerwinds B.I.S., Inc.
5690 Dehesa Rd.
El Cajon, CA 92019
(619) 445-4800

Sun Wellness, Inc.
4025 Spencer St., #104
Torrance, CA 90503
(800) 237-8400 ext. 216

Symbiotics
2301 W. Hwy 89A, Suite 107
Sedona, AZ 86336
(800) 784-4355

Tasha's Herbs
P.O. Box 9888
Jackson, WY 83002
(800) 315-0142

Whiskers Holistic Pet Products
235 East 9th St.
New York, NY 10003
(212) 979-2532

The Whole Animal Catalog
3131 Hennepin Ave. South
Minneapolis, MN 55408
(800) 377-6369

The Whole Pet, Naturally! Inc.
(800) 965-PETS

Wow-Bow Distributors, Ltd.
13B Lucon Dr.
Deer Park, NY 11729
(800) 326-0230

Young Living Essential Oils
335 Rancho Santa Fe Rd.
Encinitas, CA 92024
(760) 942-1789

Videos

Equine Massage
by Optissage

Holistic Pet Care
by Dr. Joanne Stefanatos

Interspecies Communication
by Samantha Khury

Juliette of the Herbs
by Mabinogion Films

Massage Your Dog the Lang Way and
Massage Your Cat the Lang Way
by Lang & Associates

Natural Nutrition for Dogs and Cats
by Kymythy R. Schultze,
C.C.N., A.H.I.

*The Tellington TTouch for
Happier, Healthier Dogs* and
*The Tellington TTouch for
Happier, Healthier Cats*
by Linda Tellington-Jones

❧ About the Author ❧

Kymythy R. Schultze, C.C.N., A.H.I., has been a trailblazer in the field of animal nutrition for over a decade. Her professional experience with animals includes being a trainer, a breeder, a groomer, a veterinary assistant for multiple doctors, and a wildlife rehabilitator licensed with the federal government. She has studied many holistic and allopathic modalities, including tutorage with Dr. Richard Dahout, and canine nutrition at Cornell University. She has also hosted a popular radio talk show featuring health and community service issues.

Kymythy is a certified Clinical Nutritionist and a certified Animal Health Instructor, and teaches classes in holistic care for dogs and cats at a California college and worldwide. Her nutritional recommendations are endorsed by holistic and allopathic veterinarians. She has fed her own dogs and cats a species-appropriate diet of raw foods for many years with proven results. Her breeding program has produced American and International champions; titled draft, obedience, and water rescue dogs; and, most important, nurtured beloved family companions. She has helped hundreds of people all over the world improve the health of their dogs and cats, naturally. Kymythy is also the editor of the *Holistic Dog and Cat Newsletter*, with circulation worldwide.

*"We need another and a wiser and perhaps a more
mystical concept of animals. Remote from universal nature,
and living by complicated artifice, man in civilization surveys the creature
through the glass of his knowledge and sees thereby a feather magnified
and the whole image in distortion. We patronize them for their incompleteness,
for their tragic fate of having taken form so far below ourselves.
And therein we err, and greatly err.
For the animal shall not be measured by man.
In a world older and more complete than ours
they move finished and complete, gifted with extensions of the senses
we have lost or never attained, living by voices we shall never hear.
They are not brethren, they are not underlings; they are other nations,
caught with ourselves in the net of life and time, fellow
prisoners of the splendour and travail of the earth."*

— Henry Beston